ANCIENT CULTURE AND SOCIETY

THE GREEK TRAGIC THEATRE

ANCIENT CULTURE AND SOCIETY

General Editor
M. I. FINLEY
*Professor of Ancient History
in the University of Cambridge*

A. W. H. ADKINS   Moral Values and Political
Behaviour in Ancient Greece
H. C. BALDRY   The Greek Tragic Theatre
P. A. BRUNT   Social Conflicts in the Roman Republic
M. I. FINLEY   Early Greece: the Bronze and Archaic Ages
Y. GARLAN   War in the Ancient World: A Social History
A. H. M. JONES   Augustus
G. E. R. LLOYD   Early Greeek Science: Thales to Aristotle
G. E. R. LLOYD   Greek Science After Aristotle
R. M. OGLIVIE   The Romans and Their Gods
F. H. SANDBACH   The Comic Theatre of Greece and Rome
F. H. SANDBACH   The Stoics
B. H. WARMINGTON   Nero: Reality and Legend

THE GREEK
TRAGIC THEATRE

H. C. BALDRY

*Professor of Classics at the
University of Southampton*

W · W · NORTON & COMPANY

New York · London

W. W. Norton & Company, Inc., 500 Fifth Avenue, New York, N.Y. 10110

Copyright © 1971 by H. C. Baldry

Printed in the United States of America

Library of Congress Catalog Card No. 74-128043

SBN 393-00585-2

4 5 6 7 8 9 0

CONTENTS

PLATES

Plates 1a and 1b are reproduced by permission of Miss Alison Frantz; Plate 2a by permission of Madame J. B. Serpieri (Vlasto Collection); Plate 2b by permission of The Martin von Wagner-Museum, Würzburg; Plate 3 by permission of Hirmer Fotoarchiv, München and Plate 4 by permission of The Museum of Fine Art, Boston, (Pierce Fund).

FIGURES

PREFACE

The author is indebted to Professor M. I. Finley, Mr J. W. Roberts and Dr B. A. Sparkes, who all read this book in typescript and made helpful comments. They are not, however, responsible for any of the views expressed.

Thanks are due to the following for permission to quote from copyright material: Penguin Classics for Philip Vellacott's translations of Aeschylus, E. F. Watling's translations of Sophocles and T. S. Dorsch's translation of Aristotle; Loeb Classical Library for W. S. Hett's translation of *Problems*; Chicago University Press for *Complete Greek Tragedies*, Sophocles' *Antigone*, translated by Elizabeth Wyckoff, Sophocles' *Electra*, translated by David Grene, Euripides' *Iphigenia in Tauris*, translated by Witter Bynner, and Euripides' *Electra* translated by Emily Townsend Vermeule. Other translations, except that by B. B. Rogers on page 28, are the author's own.

In addition to proper names, a small number of transliterated Greek words are used in the book. Each is explained at its first appearance, and some guidance in pronunciation is given in the index.

ANCIENT CULTURE AND SOCIETY

THE GREEK TRAGIC THEATRE

I

The Problem

IF scientists ever invent a time machine which can transport us back through history, one of the most interesting targets for our time capsule will be a theatre performance in Athens in the fifth century B.C.—the original home of Greek drama, in the period when all the tragedies now extant were first produced. In that event, much that has been written on the Greek theatre may be proved wrong—including, no doubt, a good deal of what is said in this book. But in the meantime, how far can we go towards making such a visit by scrutinising the surviving evidence and by an effort of the historical imagination? We can read the extant plays, but how far can we place them in their original historical setting? How much can we recapture of the total experience of which the texts we now possess once formed a part?

This, in its simplest terms, is the problem with which this book attempts to deal, though for reasons of space it is limited to tragedy only. The question is not one of merely antiquarian interest. The Greek tragic poets created their plays primarily for the theatre, not for readers; and the occasion, the setting, the performance, along with the words, were all interrelated aspects of the total result which the playwright had in mind. To study the text alone, from whatever point of view, is to concentrate on only part of the dramatist's creation, and always runs the risk of missing or distorting what the author intended or what his original audience got from his work. Not only archaeologists and writers on the technicalities of the Greek theatre might be proved wrong by a time machine trip to ancient Athens, but also some of those who have written on less material aspects of tragedy. It can fairly be claimed that our problem has some relevance to a number of well-worn topics with which this book does *not* deal: the religious and philo-sophical ideas of the tragic poets, for example; the origins of Attic tragedy; even that subject of unceasing controversy, the nature of tragedy itself.

To state the importance of the problem is one thing. To answer it, quite another. It may be as well to mention here at the beginning some of the difficulties which stand in the way, and which must make any answer uncertain and incomplete.

One of them is the remoteness of the ancient Greek theatre from our own experience, a fact which will stand out in every chapter that follows. In his book *On Aristotle and Greek Tragedy* Mr John Jones declares that 'probably not much of the ancient tragic experience is recoverable by us'. It is too 'desperately foreign'. The point he emphasises is true of all aspects of Greek civilisation, and of many other periods of human history. But it is no ground for a counsel of despair, that we should abandon the attempt to bridge the gap and be content (as many have been) with reinterpreting Greek drama and the rest of ancient literature to suit ourselves. Rather it is a warning against this all-too-easy approach: we should beware at every turn of the danger of reading back our own preconceptions into ancient literature, seeing Greek tragedy with twentieth-century eyes.

If the width of the gap is one difficulty, another is the deficiency of the means we possess for crossing it. For some aspects of the fifth-century theatre evidence is completely lacking; for all, after every possible source has been studied with the utmost care, the information accumulated by decades of scholarship remains woefully inadequate. In addition, each of the several types of evidence involves its own special difficulties of use and interpretation. In a short book such as this no full discussion of these complexities is possible, but in one form or another they will confront us on nearly every page. As a preliminary guide a brief account of the various kinds of information available to us is given in Chapter 2.

Remoteness from our own lives and lack or obscurity

of evidence are familiar features of any exploration of the ancient world. But the one attempted in this book has also its own particular drawbacks, which by the nature of things cannot be fully overcome. In seeking an answer to our problem we necessarily try to focus on a single point. What was it like, we ask, to be present at a performance of tragedy on such and such a day in the fifth century B.C.? A time machine might achieve a precise answer to this question, but we certainly cannot. Our information about the theatre and its uses ranges over many years, and it is a bold man who would assert —or deny—that what is proved for 450 B.C. remained true thirty years later, or that a practice known to be normal in the fourth century was also followed late in the fifth. Our picture is bound to be composite, an amalgam of items which are valid for one date or another, but perhaps never all existed together at any one time. Similarly with the plays. Each one of them, like every work of art, was a unique creation. To generalise about 'the performance of Greek tragedy' is to blur the distinction between them. For the most part fifth-century tragedy will be treated in this volume as a more or less homogeneous type. Little will be said about the various phases of its development, nor even about the differences between the three great tragic poets, Aeschylus, Sophocles and Euripides. Fortunately there is no lack of books on the individual playwrights and particular plays.

One more point, and the catalogue of difficulties is over. We are concerned with one problem, and ideally it demands one answer. The 'total experience' we are trying to recapture was a single experience. Yet our approach to it is inevitably analytical, treating it part by part and looking at one facet after another. Hence the division of the main part of this book into chapters on the city which provided the general environment for Attic drama, the dramatic festivals, the theatre, the performance, the plays that we now possess. Since all are aspects of the same whole, some overlapping between these topics is unavoidable. It is not suggested that any

3

one of them is prior to any other—that the shape of the theatre building determined the nature of the plays or vice versa, or that the environment was the cause of both. The sole essential point is that all were interconnected, and must be seen in their relation to each other. Analysis, in short, should be only the prelude to synthesis. But a book can only try to set out in readable and intelligible form the material from which the reader can draw together his own conclusion. In the last resort each of us is his own time machine.

2

The Evidence

FIRST, the extant plays.

It is easy to arrive at some conception of the number of plays produced in the fifth-century theatre at Athens. At every dramatic festival each of the three chosen tragic poets presented a trilogy—three tragedies which must have filled four hours or more of the day. A semi-comic play with a chorus of satyrs, also by the same author, followed as a short afterpiece. Comedy in its turn took the form of several single plays by different playwrights: the number varied at different periods. The total for all three types clearly adds up to hundreds; and the simplest and most sobering limitation on our knowledge and understanding of Greek drama is imposed by the fact that of all these hundreds of plays no more than a few dozen have survived. Fortunately for our purpose, the type best represented in our small collection is tragedy.

Out of all the tragedies originally performed in the fifth century B.C. we now possess thirty-two: seven by Aeschylus, seven by Sophocles, eighteen attributed (one doubtfully) to Euripides. Some we can date with certainty: official festival records were kept, and parts of their information have reached us through one means or another—in inscriptions found on the slopes of the Acropolis or elsewhere, or in statements in our manuscripts of the plays. In some plays a topical allusion points to a likely year of first performance. Others again may be put in a conjectural order on grounds of style or treatment, though a recent discovery of a scrap of papyrus has shown that conclusions reached on these lines can be as much as thirty years wrong. The safest guide where other sources are lacking seems to be study of the playwright's changing metrical technique, which has already thrown a good deal of light on the chronology of the works of Euripides. The list we arrive at by these methods is as follows:

AESCHYLUS (525–456)

Persians	472	Agamemnon	458
Seven against Thebes	467	Libation-Bearers	458
Suppliant Women		Eumenides	458
Prometheus Bound			

The trilogy produced in 458 B.C. became known as the Oresteia.

SOPHOCLES (496–406)

Ajax	Electra	
Antigone	Philoctetes	409
Women of Trachis	Oedipus at Colonus	
King Oedipus		

EURIPIDES (485–406)

Alcestis	438	The Madness of	
Medea	431	Heracles	
Hippolytus	428	Iphigenia among the	
Children of Heracles		Taurians	
Andromache		Helen	412
Hecuba		Ion	
Suppliant Women		Phoenician Women	
Electra		Orestes	408
Trojan Women	415	Iphigenia at Aulis	
		Bacchae	

Attributed to Euriphides: Rhesus

In addition to these complete texts many titles of lost tragedies are known, and thousands of 'fragments'—odd lines or parts of lines or brief passages, preserved on remnants of papyrus, or quoted for their moral sentiments or because they contain some unusual word or grammatical form. In some cases we can make a reasonable conjecture about the plot and characters of the play.

How well does all this represent the words which the fifth-century audience heard spoken or sung in the theatre of Dionysus? There was no 'publication' of the play in the modern sense: the text which the author wrote had no law of copyright to protect it, and could easily be changed or varied when copies were made. Actors, in particular, were likely to delete lines or alter them or insert new passages of their own; and it is clear that our versions are not free from 'actors' interpolations'. The deviations were stopped, we are told, by the Athenian statesman Lycurgus, who about 330 B.C. introduced a law that an official copy of the tragedies of Aeschylus, Sophocles and Euripides should be kept and read over to the actors so that they could check their texts[1]. This fourth-century authorised version may be the ultimate source from which our surviving plays come—a selection made largely for school use in Roman imperial times, though chance has added some others from an early complete edition of Euripides. The result is something very different from a random sample of fifth-century tragedy. Only the three outstanding playwrights are represented, and each of them by plays from his middle or old age: we have no complete work written by Aeschylus before he was fifty-four years old, or by Sophocles or Euripides before either was forty. Fortunately our collection includes some, at any rate, of those which were regarded as the best.

These plays were created primarily for performance, and must therefore have been performable: however strange some incidents or situations in them may seem to us, however baffling to a modern producer, they presumably contain nothing which could not be put before an audience within the limitations and conventions of the theatre of the time. But the texts themselves are uncertain guides to the way in which they were presented—how the words were spoken or sung, how actors or chorus moved, the scenery (if any) or the costumes. There are no stage directions, although it is possible that they once existed: a few, it is suspected, may have become incorporated in the spoken lines; others may be reproduced in marginal notes added at a later date ('he speaks angrily here', 'he must leap up'), but we cannot tell whether such a note reproduces an original direction or is merely an inference from the text. For the most

[1] *Lives of the Orators*, 841f. The work is attributed to Plutarch.

part we are left with whatever conclusions we ourselves can draw from the poet's own words, and here we are faced with a crucial question. When the text describes a character's appearance or a scene, was the playwright referring to what was shown by material means in the theatre, or was he appealing to the audience's imagination, using verbal description all the more fully just because what he described was *not* visible to the eye? Given the text alone, there is no means of solving this puzzle except one's own preconceptions; and we shall see what different answers these can produce. Although in a sense there can be no more reliable evidence for our purpose than the plays, the varied conclusions drawn from them by writers on the practical side of the Greek theatre show how difficult they are to use for that purpose and what treacherous guides they can be.

Second, the remains of ancient theatres; especially the theatre of Dionysus at the foot of the Acropolis in Athens, where the fifth-century tragedies were first presented. Here we can see the general shape and character of the original setting of drama; but when we look for more detail we are disappointed. The fifth-century structures in the theatre were mostly of wood, and few traces of them are left. What does survive is a complex collection of stone relics of various later stages in the theatre's history down to Roman imperial times.

Elsewhere in the Eastern Mediterranean there are many other Greek theatres dating from the fourth century B.C. or later. Some, like the outstanding example at Epidaurus, are much better preserved than their Athenian prototype and less overlaid with later changes and additions. To stand in the great Epidaurus theatre is an experience which in itself conveys some conception of Greek drama as it was originally performed. But again there is need for caution: in our search for information it is obviously dangerous to make inferences from these later sites for earlier practice at Athens.

The conclusions that can reasonably be drawn from this archaeological evidence, the idea we can form of the *place* of performance, will be discussed in greater detail in Chapter 5.

Third, ancient writers about drama and the theatre. In the modern world every aspect of theatre activity is described and discussed in print, but there was nothing of this kind in fifth-century Greece. The contemporaries of Sophocles and Euripides were greatly interested in plays, but writers at any rate took the practical side of the theatre for granted and rarely mentioned it. The earliest full description of a Greek theatre that we possess comes from a Roman—the architect and military engineer Vitruvius. In the fifth book of his Latin work *On Architecture*, published late in the first century B.C., he distinguishes 'the Greek theatre' from its Roman counterpart and describes its lay-out precisely in geometrical terms—an ideal blueprint, not a portrayal of any particular example. Two centuries later still, a longer account is given by the Greek scholar Julius Pollux, together with passages dealing in some detail with costume and masks. These two authors of Roman times, centuries remote from Periclean Athens, provide most of our explicit literary information about the theatre and its use. Until the closing years of the last century their testimony was taken as evidence relevant to the fifth-century theatre, which was therefore endowed (for example) with a stage ten or twelve feet high. Today this is seen to be impossible. It is recognised that Vitruvius and Pollux draw largely on lost writers of the 'Hellenistic' period after Alexander the Great, so that much of what they say may be true of the second century B.C. and some of it may go back to still earlier practice; but they are no longer accepted as authorities for the time of the extant tragedies. The same is true of various minor sources of a late date—short biographies of the playwrights, prefatory statements and marginal notes (known as 'scholia', by 'scholiasts') in our manuscripts of the plays, incidental comments by antiquarians and lexicographers. All these may contain some information that goes back to early origins, but how to sift the wheat from the chaff, the early from the late, is a puzzle to which there can be no sure solution.

The more we doubt this late evidence, the greater the need for scrutiny of writers closer in time to the great age of tragedy. They did not write explicitly about the theatre, but what can we read between the lines? What did they say in casual references, what did they imply or assume?

The most important contemporary source for many aspects of Greek tragedy is the surviving comedies of Aristophanes, dated between 425 and 388 B.C. One of the favourite subjects of his topical satire is the work of the tragic playwrights, especially Euripides. Anything he says or implies about the presentation of their plays is invaluable—and sometimes what he does not say is equally significant.

When we turn to the fourth century we are already moving away from the extant tragedies in time, and a question-mark hangs over any evidence we use. How far did the presentation of plays familiar to authors in this century differ from their staging in the fifth? It seems clear that the actor became more and more the centre of attention, and there was increasing emphasis on the musical side; but exactly what the differences were is an unanswerable problem. We can only be sure that the gap between fifth- and fourth-century theatre production was small when set against the contrast between both of them and the practices of Hellenistic and Roman times; nothing at all compared with the yawning abyss that separates them from theatre as we know it now. Consequently we must value any information we can glean from the fourth-century orators, or from the dialogues of Plato, who has much to say about tragedy in the *Republic* and the *Laws* and elsewhere; above all, from the principal fourth-century document concerned with drama, the *Poetics* of Aristotle, probably written soon after 335 B.C.

The importance of this brief and incomplete essay for the literary history of tragedy is obvious: to take only one point, Aristotle could read far more plays than we possess—probably all of Sophocles and Euripides ·and virtually all of Aeschylus, as well as many by other authors now lost. But one must not imagine him as merely an armchair reader of drama, sitting in the library of his philosophical school and toiling over his play-collection. For Aristotle, as one of his editors says, 'a tragedy is essentially something to be acted'. During his many years at Athens he must often have been present at the dramatic festivals, witnessing all those aspects of the performance—the spectacle, the setting, the music, the dance—of which we know so little. No one who reads his biological works can doubt that he would be a more observant theatre-goer than most. It is true that little of this background of experience emerges explicitly in the *Poetics*. Aristotle never describes the presentation of plays. What we get from him is (unfortunately) not description of theatrical practices, but tantalising reference and allusion: the rest is taken for granted as something familiar to all. But there is a point too often ignored which will be emphasised in this book: that underlying all he says about drama in the *Poetics* is a set of assumptions about its presentation; and if the picture we reconstruct from the rest of our evidence runs contrary to those assumptions, it is unlikely to be right.

Fourth, what are commonly called the 'monuments': vase-paintings, sculptures and statuettes, various other works of art which appear to depict some aspect of what was done in the theatre. Fresh discoveries in recent times have added to this mass of material until it now contains many hundred items. Its emergence has made scholars reconsider their attitude to the rest of the

evidence, and has done more in this century than anything else to change our conception of Greek drama
as it was originally performed.

Here again there are problems, some of which are not
likely to be solved. Many items in the list can be given
an approximate date and attributed to a definite source
—sometimes, even to a named artist; but there are others
which cannot, and until we know their date and where
they came from their relevance to fifth-century Athens is
hard to judge. Even when time and place of origin are
known, the same question arises as over the literary
evidence. How much can a picture drawn in 350 B.C. tell
us about theatre production in the time of Sophocles?
How far is a scene on a vase from the Greek communities
in Southern Italy valid testimony for the use of the
theatre at Athens? 'Monuments' of much later periods,
like the writings of Vitruvius and Pollux, have now been
largely discounted as evidence: we no longer think that
a statuette of the second century A.D. is useful information about the tragic actor's costume six hundred years
before. But for earlier work the point is more problematic, and the question of the time and distance gap
has to be looked at afresh in every case.

There are other difficulties besides this, especially in
dealing with vase-paintings. Often they portray a scene
which might come from a play, but we cannot decide
whether the figures in it are costumed actors or the
characters of the story as the artist imagined them. In
other instances connection with the theatre is certain:
the figures wear or hold masks, or a flute-player is there
to symbolise the fact that this is a play. But even here
what we have before us is very different from a photo-
graph. On the one hand, what the artist shows us is
limited by the space available and the conventions of
his technique. On the other, no realistic precision re-
stricts his imagination: he may add to his picture human
or divine beings who were not in the play, put into a
theatre setting incidents which were narrated in a
messenger's speech, turn the mask into an expressive
face so that we see partly the actor, partly the character

he represents. We must not treat as a factual record the artist's half-realised effort to express what was in his mind.

One last comment may be added as postscript to this brief and perhaps depressing survey. Where the handling of evidence of all types is so fraught with difficulty, it may well seem that the pursuit of truth is likely to be hopeless; and if each type were completely separate from the rest, this would be so. But conclusions can be reached by comparison across the field—by seeking out every link that can be found between the text of the plays, the other literary evidence, the remains of the theatre, and the 'monuments'. In a short book it is obviously impracticable to give reasons for every statement, but where possible an attempt will be made to reveal the grounds as well as the conclusions—to illustrate, at least, how the complex evidence that is available can be used.

3

The City

THE social context that gave birth to the extant tragedies was the city of Athens in the most remarkable years of her history: her leadership of the Greek states in the defeat of the Persian invaders, commemorated in Aeschylus' *Persians*, the earliest of the plays; the transformation of leadership into imperial power under the guidance of Pericles; the disastrous Peloponnesian War against Sparta and her allies (431–404 B.C.) which is reflected in some of the plays of Euripides. The splendour of the city's public places was evidence to all comers of her greatness and prosperity: the temples on the Acropolis, the civic buildings in the market-place, the theatre.

The glory that was Athens. But to realise her achievement fully it is important to get the scale right. By modern standards this was not a large city. Population estimates vary, but the total for Athens and her surrounding territory, Attica, can never have been much above 300,000 in this period; and of these probably less than half lived in the city itself. There is no parallel in our time for so much creative activity by a community of this size. In the field of drama the contrast is particularly marked. How is it that whereas modern cities in this population bracket pull their theatres down or struggle to keep them going, in the theatre at Athens vast audiences watched the production of hundreds of new plays? Various aspects of the city's life supply a partial answer—politics, wealth, education, religion; but each must be seen in its ancient setting if its place in the background to the Greek theatre is to be understood.

Athens, we are told, was a democracy; and Pericles himself, in the famous funeral speech put into his mouth by the historian Thucydides, couples the assertion with

14

a picture of a democratic community surpassing all others in the practice of the arts (II, 40, 41). 'We are lovers of the beautiful . . . Athens is the school of Greece.' If we consider the population as a whole, the claim to be a democracy will not bear examination. Something like half of the total were slaves, entirely devoid of political rights. Perhaps twenty or thirty thousand were 'metics', non-Athenians who lived in Attica and had certain rights, but no full citizenship. The rest were the citizens and their families: the adult male citizen body to which in any sense the term 'democracy' could apply numbered at most 40,000. Even within this group dividing lines were drawn—not only the formal division into 'tribes' and the geographical division into parishes or 'demes', but also a hierarchy of classes based on wealth; less definite but no less important, strong prejudice in favour of high birth, which through most of the fifth century B.C. gave the leadership in most spheres of life to men of good family. All this must be set against Athens' claim to be a democratic state. Yet it remains true (and all-important for the study of the Attic theatre) that Athens was a more compact, more integrated society than the democracies of today. Among its citizens there is little sign of the we–they antithesis which brings apathy to the life of so many modern communities. The decision-making parliament was no remote body, but a mass meeting in the heart of the city which all citizens could, and a large proportion did, attend. Any citizen could be chosen to play a larger part for a limited time, whether as a member of the Council of Five Hundred or as a holder of high (or not so high) office. Of course there were means by which much of the real power was retained in certain hands; but the whole citizen body could feel that it participated directly in the running of its affairs. We shall find obvious parallels between the meetings of the Assembly on the Pnyx and the performances in the theatre half a mile away: the involvement of the mass audience, the active participation of a large number of the citizens, the eloquence of the orators and of the actors.

On the financial side, the ancient Greek city has been well described as a closed private corporation administered for the benefit of its citizens, who were both its managers and its shareholders; again a form of organisation in which all could take part. Naturally the wealth so administered had much to do with the pre-eminence of Athens in the arts. Not that the ordinary Greek city-state was wealthy by modern standards: its agriculture was primitive, its trade small-scale, its warfare murderous but inefficient. Ancient Greece as a whole was an underdeveloped area compared even with Rome a few centuries later. But Athens in the fifth century B.C. did accumulate relatively great wealth as the contributions of her allies towards joint defence against Persia became converted into virtual tribute from subject states; and some of her individual citizens did achieve relatively great riches, from which they were obliged to contribute to the common good. The significant point for our purpose is how the city's wealth was spent: how large a portion of it was given (no doubt, partly for reasons of prestige) to the splendour of public buildings like the Parthenon or the magnificence of public occasions. We shall see later what share of their finances the citizen-body devoted to the dramatic festivals.

Expenditure of money on the arts surely implies enthusiasm for the arts. Was the background to this, as we might tend to assume, a high level of education? Not if by this we mean the level of literacy or numeracy aimed at in developed countries today; still less if we are thinking of the absorption of specialised knowledge. Specialisation on anything like the modern scale was unknown in Periclean Athens. Even books (rolls of papyrus) and reading played little part in life, though there is some evidence for their spread towards the end of the century. What mattered was the spoken word, the use of the human voice as a means of communication or persuasion or entertainment; and in this, though not in literacy or knowledge, the ancient Athenians had the advantage over the comparatively inarticulate creature that is modern man. Brilliant utilisation of the spoken

16

word, mostly in the open air, was the central feature both of their vivid but erratic politics and of what we now misleadingly call their 'literature'. Most of the 'literary' genres which the Greeks created sprang from types of occasion involving speech or song: epic, for example, from recital before feasting nobles or festival crowds; oratory, from political debate in the assembly or from the law courts; the philosophic dialogue, from conversation in the market-place or the wrestling-school; drama, from the festivals of Dionysus in his open-air theatre. Within drama, as we shall see in more detail in a later chapter, each of the main uses of words—narrative, persuasive rhetoric, argument, song—had its place in the pattern that made up a play.

The mention of Dionysus has brought the gods into the picture. No account of the background of Greek drama or any other aspect of Greek life can be complete without them. The thought of them roused different reactions on different occasions and among different sections of the population—fear, wonder, laughter, scepticism, rarely love. But they were continually present in the Greek mind as religion is not in the mind of the modern man. Their powers and arbitrary actions were his explanation of most of what happened in the world about him, which we seek to understand through science. Their ritual was an essential part of his daily life. Even enlightened Athens was dominated by Athena's great temple. It is not surprising that Attic drama should be closely bound up with the worship of a deity, or that the gods should figure so prominently in the plays.

Plato in his *Republic* turns against the importance given to the theatre in Athens, and proposes to expel the playwrights along with other poets from his ideal city. Commentators through the ages have not been slow to attack this remarkable proposal, but one significant aspect of it is often overlooked: the philosopher's assumption that poetry, especially dramatic poetry, requires treatment at length in a discussion of the ideal state, his belief that the writers of tragedy and comedy are such a powerful influence on the community that

17

they are *worth* expelling. The *Republic*, though written twenty or thirty years after the death of Sophocles and Euripides, is the most striking evidence we have for the point which has been the main burden of this chapter: that drama flourished and rose to such heights of achievement in fifth-century Athens because it was not a fringe activity in a loosely knit society, but occupied a central place in the existence and thoughts—and the financial outlay—of a compact community. In the next chapter a closer look at the dramatic festivals will show more clearly the part played by the theatre in the city's life.

4

The Festivals

could be my conclusion

THE festival of the arts is a familiar feature of our own time. From Edinburgh to Salzburg, from Stratford, Ontario to Sydney, festivals flourish and attract visitors in their thousands; and in the great majority, plays of one sort or another have a prominent place. We are in a better position than our grandfathers to understand the festival as one of the ways in which drama can reach the public; even to grasp that in fifth-century Greece it could be *the* way. But there are differences between the dramatic festivals of Athens and our own which make our twentieth-century experience only partly relevant.

One feature, not unknown today but far more prominent in Greece, is the element of competition in the ancient festivals. Most aspects of Greek life were strongly influenced by the idea of competition—not for profit, but for prestige, repute, glory. The rivalry between the heroes in the *Iliad* sets a pattern which is reflected later in peacetime activities as well as war: not only athletic contests at the Games, but contests between 'rhapsodes' in the recitation of Homer, between playwrights and between actors in the theatre. As we shall see, the competitive side of the dramatic festivals played a large part in shaping their organisation.

A still more important point, foreign to most theatre festivals in our own time, is that the Attic festivals were religious—some of the many occasions in honour of the gods which punctuated the year. Athena, the city's own patron goddess whose giant statue stood in the Parthenon on the Acropolis, had her great summer festival at which the epics of Homer were recited. The turn of drama came in the winter and early spring at celebrations for Dionysus, also called Bacchus, whose main home in Athens—his temple and his theatre—lay below the

19

Acropolis at its south-eastern corner. For us a theatre is far from being holy ground, and the conception of it as the precinct of a god is strange indeed. But no Greek questioned it; and among all their deities none was more suited for this function than Dionysus. He was far more than the god of wine. He was a god of fertility and growth, whose animal incarnations were the bull and the goat; his symbols were the luxuriantly growing ivy and the phallus. His ritual—a favourite subject with the vase-painters—was mostly performed by women: through dance and wine it could lead to a state of ecstasy which brought joy to the worshippers and a sense of possession by the god. But the Greeks' conception of him had also its grim and gruesome side. Dark stories were told such as Euripides dramatises in his *Bacchae*—legends of the fate of those who resisted the god, torn to pieces on the mountains by his frenzied women devotees. Here was a deity whose realm was passion rather than intellect, joy and horror rather than reason, one to whom both tragedy and comedy could belong; and although for the fifth-century Athenian the wild orgies in the hills were no more than a tale and Dionysus was now accepted into the company of the Olympians, there was still a spirit about his cult which set him apart from the other gods and must have given his festivals an atmosphere of their own.

The religious character of Greek festivals does not mean that they were cut off from the general life of the community, as might be supposed in these secular days; least of all, where the god was so close to the heart of the people as Dionysus. The thought of a religious ceremony in a thronged cathedral in medieval times may bring us nearer to the truth. Or for a comparison in population-involvement (but without the god) we may turn to a crowded football match in a modern city—with a higher proportion of the citizens present. But there is in fact no parallel in medieval or modern times to the ancient situation. We can best get a conception of the scale of the Dionysiac festivals and their impact on the community by looking at some aspects of our

20

information about them: the programme of events, t
administration and (always an illuminating item in
theatre history) finance.

Of the various festivals of Dionysus in the Attic calendar one, the oldest, probably had no connection with drama in the fifth century B.C.: the Anthesteria, held about the end of February when the jars of wine from the last autumn's grapes were opened. Those at which plays were performed took place at times of year which are to us surprising. Even in Mediterranean countries open-air theatre is not now a winter pastime; further north it flourishes only in the best of summers. Yet in the districts of Attica outside the city, as we shall see later, the normal time for drama contests was late December; while in Athens itself competitions were held at the Lenaea about the end of January. Even the City Dionysia, the most important of all, came as early in the spring as the last week of March, when in modern Greece the tourist season has hardly begun. No doubt there were religious reasons for this timing; but considering the scale of the festivals and the number of citizens actively involved, we must also see their dates as part of the general activity pattern of the Athenian year. Spring and summer were the period for trade, for travel; above all, for war. From spring to autumn, if Attica was free from invasion, there was busy work on the land: the soil was prepared and the seed sown in autumn, the harvest gathered in early summer. The winter, while campaigning was at a standstill and the seed grew, was the time most free for Dionysus and his festivals, as well as the season when they were most needed; and the finest fruit of the winter's theatre work, of all the preparations and rehearsals, came naturally at the City Dionysia at the beginning of spring.

Of the Lenaea, so called from one of the names given to women worshippers of the god, little need be said. Our knowledge of its ritual is slight, but it certainly

procession through the streets and dramatic
early days, held in a precinct of the god
enaeon, but transferred (perhaps in the mid-
....y) to the theatre south-east of the Acropolis.
The evidence of inscriptions suggests that official competitions in tragedy and comedy started at the Lenaea
about 440 B.C. But comedy predominated: in the fifth
century only two tragic poets competed annually at this
festival with two plays each, and the most famous rarely
took part.

The Lenaea was a domestic affair, celebrated when
the Aegean was stormy and there was no influx from
other states—a local gathering which would relish to the
full the local and personal satire of an Aristophanes. But
when the City Dionysia began the sailing season had
started and Athens, if war did not prevent it, was
thronged with visitors—merchants who came for trade,
representatives of the 'allies' bringing tribute, travellers
eager to see the wonders of the finest city of Greece or
drawn there by the festival itself. This was the 'Great'
Dionysia or just the Dionysia, an occasion in a sense Pan-
Hellenic, which brought not only the Athenians but
people from all over the Greek-speaking world into the
theatre. This was the main setting of tragedy; and because of its importance far more information has reached
us about it than about the Lenaea, whether in inscriptions or literary references or the commentators. For
both reasons an account of the City Dionysia must be the
central subject of this chapter. Many details are unknown to us and many points are open to dispute, including the order of events; but they have little effect on
our idea of the occasion as a whole, and it will be enough
for our purpose to reconstruct what seems a likely
picture, from the preliminaries months beforehand
(probably the previous midsummer) to the contest itself.

The community was involved from the first through
its nominal head, the 'Archon' who gave his name to the

22

year for which he held office—not a leading politician or professional civil servant (though he was paid) but an ordinary citizen chosen by lot from all except the lowest income-group; the nearest thing in Athens to the Mayor of a modern English town. Running the Dionysia was one of his many duties. To him the poets wishing to compete 'applied for a chorus', and for tragedy he selected three. Each had to put forward a group of new plays, three tragedies and an afterpiece; except that after the death of Aeschylus in 456 B.C. he was paid the remarkable tribute that anyone offering plays by him for the contest was given a place.

We do not know how the Archon made his choice or whose advice he sought. He had two assistants, but they were for all his work and had no theatre expertise. (No suggestion here of a professional Director whose verdict should be free from national or municipal control!) It seems unlikely that such a busy official read plays in order to reach his decision, although a passage in Plato (*Laws* 817d) suggests that each poet may have read to him specimens of his work. Probably he chose playwrights rather than plays, and largely by repute. As the selection in one year of a certain Gnesippus in preference to Sophocles shows, he could make mistakes; and we shall see that there was an opportunity for him to be called to account.

To present plays costs money; and in ancient Greece no one imagined that the theatre could or should pay its way. A further duty of the Archon was to initiate the financing of the contest by finding for each playwright a *choregos* or promoter—a patron, if patronage can be compulsory; a surtax-payer, if taxation can be a path to glory. (In some inscriptions, the name of the *choregos* is placed before that of the poet.) Providing money for a production at the Dionysia, like maintaining a warship for a year or paying for a delegation to another state, was seen as a service which the rich could be expected to give to the city. Some well-to-do citizens volunteered—a sure means to popularity. More often, we may suspect, the Archon had to exercise his power of nomination: if his nominee had performed no such public service for a year, he could escape only by challenging a man he claimed to be still wealthier, who must then either take over the expense or exchange properties—or fight the matter out in the courts. The playwright's luck in the allocation of *choregoi*, probably settled by lot, was all-important for his prospects in the contest. Law prescribed a minimum outlay, but the promoter's willingness or unwillingness to go beyond it could make bad plays a success or good ones a failure. Nicias, the popular statesman who owned a thousand slaves and made a handsome income by hiring them out for work in the silver-mines, never failed to win the prize.

The simplicity of the presentation of plays and the absence of specialisation eliminated some of the expenses that burden the modern theatre. There was no lighting, little or no scenery, few properties. Most of the functions now divided between several individuals—author, director, composer, choreographer—were combined in the person of the poet, who not only wrote the text, but composed the music for the songs and devised the dances. In the fifth century he generally trained the chorus himself. But there were other aspects of the production that bore heavily on the *choregos*. He had to find and pay the chorus of fifteen, and probably the flute-player also. Occasionally a second chorus was required; and for all there were masks and costumes to be provided (an opportunity to cut expenses here, by hiring them second-hand), not to mention a party after the contest was over. When late in the century the practice arose of employing a professional chorus-trainer, there was his salary to pay as well. A particularly variable item in the budget was the provision of non-speaking 'extras': some star actors demanded a spectacular retinue.

But what of the actors themselves?

For each play, as we shall see in more detail later, three were needed: a first, second and third actor who by changes of mask and costume divided the speaking parts between them. The first playwrights had acted in their own plays, and later they employed actors of their own choosing; but by about the middle of the fifth century the Archon had probably come into the picture here too, selecting three state-paid star actors, 'protagonists', for the contest in tragedy and allocating them to the poets by lot—though appearance as the star in four plays on end may seem an unlikely feat. (There is no evidence for the existence of a prompter.) How the second and third actors were chosen or paid we do not know: possibly by the protagonist himself. In the fourth century, if not earlier, an actor who was engaged for the festival and failed to appear was fined by the state.

One more official preliminary was necessary some time before the festival: preparation for the selection of the judges (Greek: *kritai*, whence our word 'critic'). The whole process leading up to a verdict in the contests was complicated by precautions against corruption, and our evidence (mainly from the fourth century orators) leaves some points uncertain and obscure: there is nothing to show, for example, whether the same judges acted in all the festival contests or a separate group for each. But the first steps towards appointing them seem clear. To make sure that the whole citizen body was represented the ten 'tribes' into which it was divided were taken as a basis, and from each the Council drew up a list of names. On what ground individuals were put on the list we do not know: there is no evidence that experience of drama or critical acumen were taken into account. Perhaps more relevant is the fact that the *choregoi* were present, and apparently did their best to get their supporters included. Once the names were decided, they were placed in ten urns, one for each tribe; and these were sealed by the presidents of the Council and by the *choregoi*, and deposited with the public treasurers in the Acropolis till the contest was due. To tamper with them in the meantime was a capital offence.

News of all these preparations must have been common knowledge in the city: in a society without printing or newspapers, information (reliable or otherwise) would have other means of circulating—especially such contentious items as the choice of playwrights and actors and *choregoi*. Nevertheless, a day or two before the festival an official ceremony, the *proagon*, was held which in effect gave the public full details of the programme—in the second half of the fifth century, in Pericles' new hall, the Odeum, built next to the theatre. Here came the chosen poets with their *choregoi*, actors, musicians and chorus members, splendidly dressed and wearing garlands; and each poet in turn appears to have mounted the platform with his actors and announced the titles of his plays, or possibly even a brief summary of the plot. No masks or theatrical costumes were worn, so that the identity of the masked figures to be watched later in the theatre could be known to all.

Another act of preparation was necessary before the festival could begin: to ensure the presence of the god— for the City Dionysia, Dionysus Eleuthereus, so called because his cult and his image were said to have been brought to Athens from Eleutherae, near the north-west border of Attica. Normally the image stood in the temple in the theatre precinct. Now, to re-enact his coming, it was taken to a shrine at the outskirts of the city on the road to Eleutherae and carried back by torchlight to be placed in the theatre.

On the first day of the festival itself the whole city was on holiday: even prisoners were released on bail. The proceedings opened in the morning with the full pomp and ceremony of a great procession through the streets, with dancing and the singing of satirical songs on the way. Girls of high birth bore golden baskets of offerings. There were citizens in white and metics in scarlet, and the *choregoi* in robes of special splendour. Huge phalluses were carried to symbolise the god's good gift of fertility, and a bull and other animals were led along ready for sacrifice when the long column reached the theatre precinct.

This was the starting point for several days of contests, the exact arrangement of which is unknown to us. They were not all in drama, but included a competition between choruses from the ten 'tribes' in the performance of 'dithyrambs', sung and danced in honour of the

26

god. Ten choruses of men took part, and ten of boys; and there were fifty in each. For this contest also *choregoi* and poets (sometimes well-known figures from other states, like Simonides or Pindar) and flute-players and trainers were involved; but the performers wore no masks, and whatever part the dithyramb may have played in the origins of tragedy, it falls itself outside the scope of our theme.

With the dramatic contests came the climax of the festival. They began with items which to us, who see drama as a thing apart, seem a strange prelude to the presentation of plays. A sucking-pig was sacrificed to purify the theatre, and libations were poured. This was the time of year when the 'allies' brought their tribute to Athens; and now a line of young Athenians marched across in front of the audience, each carrying one silver talent in a jar to show the balance of tribute over expenditure for the past year. Announcements were made of honours conferred on citizens or strangers for services to the city. The sons of men who had died in battle for Athens paraded in armour given them by the state and listened to a short exhortation before going to the special seats allotted to them. Perhaps last came the completion of the selection of the judges: the ten urns, now brought down to the theatre from the Acropolis, were unsealed, the Archon drew one name from each, and the ten thus chosen swore to give an impartial verdict.

These solemn ceremonies were the immediate context for the opening tragedy. The order of performance between the competitors had already been settled by lot; to be last seems to have been regarded as the best. A trumpet sounded, and the first play began. In years of peace this was the starting point for four days of drama: probably three on which groups of tragedies with their satyr-drama afterpieces were presented, and one filled by five comedies. During the Peloponnesian War time and expense were saved by reducing the days to three, each with tragedies and afterpiece in the morning and a single comedy in the afternoon. Some lines from the *Birds* of Aristophanes are our evidence, in which his feathered chorus points out to the audience one of the advantages of having wings (786–9). In Rogers' Gilbertian translation:

> Only fancy, dear spectators, had you each a brace of wings,
> Never need you, tired and hungry, at a Tragic Chorus stay.
> You would likely, when it bored you, spread your wings and fly away,
> Back returning, after luncheon, to enjoy our Comic Play.

The presentation of the tragedies and the audience's reactions to them will be the subject of the next two chapters. Our picture of the festival programme of events can be completed here with some account of how it closed.

At the end of the contest came the verdict: each of the ten judges wrote his order of preference on a tablet; and when the tablets had been put in an urn, the Archon drew out five of them and on these the issue was decided. The names of the victorious poet and *choregos* were announced, and the Archon crowned them in the theatre with crowns of ivy. How the prize for acting was awarded our evidence does not reveal, but it did not necessarily go to the protagonist in a victorious play. Victors' celebrations must have followed, and we may imagine the triumphant procession that escorted *choregos* and poet and protagonist home. Afterwards the winning *choregos* in the tragic contest would put up a tablet to commemorate his success, and the actor might dedicate his mask to the god.

The final event of the festival period underlines again the concern of the whole community with the Dionysia: one more gathering of the citizens was held in the theatre, this time for a special Assembly to review the festival. The Archon's management of the whole occasion was discussed, and he and other officials might be complimented and honoured—or, on occasion, attacked. Complaints were raised of misconduct or even violence during the procession or the contests: if the Assembly gave them support, the sequel might well be an action in

28

the courts. In 349 B.C. the great orator Demosthenes claimed that he had been struck in the theatre while acting as *choregos*; and although the matter was settled by compromise and the speech *Against Midias* which he prepared was never delivered, it still survives as one of our sources of evidence about the festival.

From first to last it is obvious that the festivals of Dionysus had a very different place in the life of Athens from any form of drama today. The point can be made more precise by considering two aspects of the City Dionysia in more detail—the numbers of people and the sums of money involved.

Remarkable in itself is the number of active participants, mostly drawn not from a separate professional class but from various points in the social spectrum. No doubt actors, musicians and trainers were specialised 'theatre people', and so in a sense were the poets; but in the fifth century at any rate this cannot have been true of the chorus-members, who for all three contests—dithyramb, tragedy and comedy—probably numbered nearly twelve hundred. Financial backing came from men of wealth and influence; ritual was in the hands of the priests; organisation and judging lay with ordinary citizens, from the Archon downwards, who had greatness thrust upon them. If we add 'extras', stage-hands, wardrobe assistants and the like, the total actively concerned must have been not far short of 1500—apart from the many others who took part in ceremonies or processions.

How many came to watch and listen? Inevitably, a great multitude. This was a day of ritual in honour of a popular god; the only chance, moreover, to see the play in the city. Although repetition of works of Aeschylus was allowed after his death and after the fifth century, as we shall see, other revivals were included in the contest, there was never any possibility of a play having a 'run' in the modern sense. The performance was unique, and the auditorium had to be large enough to hold the vast crowd of those who wanted to take part in this one occasion and watch this single presentation of the play. The question of its exact total capacity is difficult. The number of people occupying a telephone kiosk can vary from one to twenty-six, according to whether they want to use the telephone or to advertise a student rag. The number that sat on a bench in the theatre of Dionysus would vary with the weather or with popular expectation about the plays; and in addition it is uncertain how far accommodation for the audience reached up the slope of the Acropolis in the late fifth century B.C. If we take the most likely view on this issue and allow individuals sixteen inches each (surely near the minimum), the result is about 17,000. Yet in our sole piece of literary evidence, a passage of Plato's *Symposium* (175e), the poet Agathon is said to have won the prize for tragedy in 416 B.C. before 'more than 30,000'. Probably the phrase is colloquial exaggeration—though one must bear the telephone kiosk in mind! The modern theatre-goer may well wonder whether the capacity audience of 17,000 was often reached; but repeated enlargements to the auditorium and references to struggles for seats suggest that the theatre was usually full.

The composition of this vast throng was as varied as Greek society itself. At the front in seats of honour were many whose presence marked this as a great civic and religious occasion: priests, Archons and other holders of public office, benefactors of the city, the sons of men killed in battle, ambassadors from other Greek states. All these were ceremoniously conducted to their places. In the theatre as it stands today there are sixty seats in the front row inscribed with titles, and others further back. Most of the inscriptions date from Roman times, but many are carved over similar previous markings and the array of notables which they suggest cannot have been very different in earlier days. In the middle of the front row the finely carved throne of the priest of Dionysus Eleuthereus, probably a copy of a fourth-century original, recalls a splendid moment in Aristophanes' *Frogs* (405 B.C.). Dionysus, on his way to Hades where he will act as judge himself in a tragic poets' contest, appeals in a moment of panic to his own priest for help (297):

My priest, protect me! We'll have a drink together afterwards.

These places were 'complimentaries': whether their holders were given tickets we do not know. Admission to the rest of the theatre was probably by ticket: small coin-like discs of lead have survived which may be seat-tokens. The price seems to have been the same for all parts of the theatre—two obols (a third of a drachma) per day; but from the time of Pericles the state treasury paid for the seats of citizens. The money went to a lessee who made a contract with the state for the theatre's mainten-ance and repair. This two-obol payment from the treasury has often been regarded as a form of 'dole', but it has another aspect: the assumption that drama is the community's concern, as we think education is today.

Citizens, no doubt, were the mass of the audience, especially as they were admitted free. Special areas were reserved for members of the Council and for the *epheboi*, the young men under military training: attend-ance at the festival was one of their duties. It seems likely that each of the ten 'tribes' had its own block of seats, but as there were thirteen blocks the arrangement is not clear. Metics must have been there in large numbers: many of them could well afford to pay. There were hundreds, if not thousands, of visitors from other states, possibly seated at the sides of the auditorium.

A good deal of argument has raged over the question whether women and children were present: if they were admitted for the tragedies they must also have been there for the comedies, at any rate in the war years when all were on the same day; and this is a thought which an earlier generation of scholars found difficult to accept. Many passages of comedy imply that the great majority of the audience were men, but there is evidence enough to make it likely that in the late fifth century and the fourth some women were in the theatre for tragedy and

31

comedy alike; and there is no reason to doubt that this was true earlier as well. On the other hand the belief that women sat separately from the men rests on very dubious grounds, and probably the free women at any rate sat with their menfolk. Even members of that still humbler section of Athenian society, the slaves, were allowed admission; but only, one suspects, when brought by their masters, just as in countries were segregation is the rule a coloured servant may be with her employer's children on a 'white' beach. At the end of the fourth century Theophrastus includes among his *Characters* (9) a 'shameless' man who takes a slave attendant along with his sons into the theatre and puts them into seats he bought for visitors.

Audience figures are one criterion of a community's interest in drama. Another is the amount of financial support that it receives. The size of the Arts Council budget and the meagre municipal expenditure on theatre are all too significant for Britain today; and so also is the fate of such subsidies in an economic crisis. Is it possible to apply any such test to ancient Athens?

There are many difficulties in the way. The relevant information is slight and conflicting, and much of it comes from sources where stating a case is more important than the truth. Even if we knew much more, the great difference of financial systems would rule out any close comparison with the modern situation. But with a wide margin of error the sum can be done and a very rough idea of Athenian expenditure on the Dionysiac festivals can be reached.

In a court case (XXI, 1–4) the speech-writer Lysias makes the plaintiff describe his outlay on services to the state during the last years of the fifth century B.C. He speaks of spending 30 minas as *choregos* for tragedy (1 talent = 60 minas = 6000 drachmas), 16 as *choregos* for comedy, and in the dithyrambic contest 50 minas on a men's chorus, 15 on a chorus of boys. He may well be exaggerating to improve his case, and he claims to have spent four times the legal minimum; on the other hand, this was during the years of financial stress not long before Athens' defeat. About 388 B.C. another client of Lysias gives 50 minas as the cost of acting twice as tragic *choregos* (XIX, 42). Such figures suggest that through this method of surtax something like 6 talents was spent on the City Dionysia.

As to the direct outlay from state funds, expenditure on seats for citizens must have amounted to at least 3 talents, minus any payment that was made by the lessee of the theatre to the treasury. The sums paid to the actors are not known, but can hardly have totalled less than a talent; and at least as much must be allowed for the competing poets, who all received money 'honoraria' apart from the ivy crown. For state and *choregoi* together 11 talents may be taken as a very approximate figure. But this is for the contests alone: the total for the festival as a whole must have been a good deal higher, and there is the Lenaea to add. The German scholar Boeckh estimated direct Athenian state expenditure on all festivals at 25 to 30 talents a year.

How much was a talent? To express its worth in modern currency is impossible; but some idea of its value may be gained from the rough calculation that it would keep fifteen or more families of four for a year at the subsistence level at which most Athenians lived; or it would buy perhaps thirty slaves at average prices. Halve these figures, and we have what a *choregos* for tragedy might spend.

How did all this compare with the city's total revenues or her other expenditures? Outlay on the equivalent of police has been estimated at 40 talents a year. 'Defence' costs fluctuated violently according to the needs of wars, and so did the amount coming into the treasury: a figure mentioned for the eve of the Peloponnesian War is 'not less than a thousand talents a year' (Xenophon, *Anabasis* VII, 1, 27). Most of this sum—a vast one by the standards of the time—came from the 'allies'. It was the city's imperial power, while it lasted, that made her splendour possible, including the splendour of her festivals, although as *choregoi* her rich citizens made their contribution too. For the future of drama the point was vital: expenditure on the Dionysia does not seem to have been greatly cut in the hard closing years of the war, although the contests were shortened; but when defeat had come and the tribute payments had ended, the theatre suffered along with the rest of the city and lost some of the magnificence of its fifth-century days.

So far this chapter has been concerned with the festivals at Athens, and above all with the Great Dionysia in the spring. Because the nature of our information makes this stand out in the centre of the scene, it is easy to assume that only the theatre by the Acropolis mattered—a small-scale parallel to the modern dramatic critic's tendency to concentrate on a capital city like London and ignore what goes on elsewhere. But this was far from all. To complete our description something must be said of a more obscure aspect of the picture: the festivals held in Attica outside the city, commonly given the misleading name of the 'Rural' Dionysia (the Greek means 'in the fields' as distinct from 'in the town'). Here we know nothing of audience figures or financial outlay. Our scraps of evidence come mainly from the fourth century B.C. or later, but what they suggest is probably not far wrong for the closing decades of the fifth.

Every village or township (*demos*) of Attica held its own festival for Dionysus, normally in December. When the farmer-hero of Aristophanes' *Acharnians* makes his one-man peace with Sparta, he celebrates with a procession in which his daughter represents the girls bearing offerings to the gods, two slaves carry a phallus on a pole, and the farmer in place of a gay chorus sings a hymn while his wife (the spectators) looks on from the roof. This is the customary fertility ritual in miniature, reduced to its simplest form. But it is clear that in many 'demes' the procession was combined, as in the city, with dramatic contests more or less on the Athenian model. A fifth-century inscription from the small village of Icarion (the modern Dionyso) shows that it also had its *choregoi*. Traces of theatres are few: the most complete, at Thoricus in the south-east, seems to have been a small and simple affair compared with the great theatre below the Acropolis. But the theatre which Thucydides (VIII, 93) mentions at the Piraeus, then as now the port of Athens, must have been large; we know that ambassadors from other states attended the Piraeus festival, which may have been little less splendid than the City Dionysia itself. Euripides is said to have competed there.

One inscription (*I.G.ii²*, 3090) has been interpreted as recording that plays by Sophocles and Aristophanes were victorious at Eleusis, near the western border of Attica; but this probably refers to the revival of plays already performed at Athens, a custom which may have been common at the 'Rural' Dionysia in the fifth century as it was throughout Greece in later years. It is tempting to trace back into the fifth century the practice which is clear from the orators in the fourth—'touring' of the 'demes' by companies of actors in well-known plays by the great masters of tragedy. With so many opportunities available some people seem to have become habitual theatre-goers. Early in the fourth century Plato described these 'theatre-fans and music-lovers' in the *Republic* (475d): in their enthusiasm 'they run round the city and country Dionysia, never missing a festival, as if they were under contract to listen to every performance'. For a minority in ancient Attica, as in the modern world, drama could become a consuming enthusiasm, a nearly continuous activity. But its distinctive place in the life of Athens was the one described in most of this chapter— not the favourite pastime of the few, but a great civic and religious occasion for the community as a whole, rich in pomp and ceremony, financed from the public treasury and from private wealth, involving hundreds of participants, attended by many thousands; a central event in the year, which not even the stresses of war and defeat could stop.

5

The Theatre

WITHIN the great festival of Dionysus at Athens (Fig. 1) we are chiefly concerned with the days of drama; in particular, with the performance of the tragedies. But there is a preliminary question. In every country and every age (including our own) the presentation of plays is closely related to the place where it is done. What do we know of the details of the theatre by the Acropolis at the time when the extant tragedies were first produced?

If we look down at the theatre as it exists today (Plate 1a), what we see is confused—and confusing. The lower part of the long slope from the Acropolis rock is covered with curving tiers of stone benches, many of them incomplete. At the bottom is the semi-circular row of marble thrones already mentioned in the last chapter; and beyond them, surrounded by a low barrier of upright marble slabs, lies a flat semi-circle paved with marble: in the centre of it a large diamond-shaped pattern catches the eye. In the middle of the straight side of the paved area stands a flight of five stone steps, and from this to the right-hand edge runs a line of masonry a few feet high, supported by sculptured figures most of which are headless. Beyond this are lines of stone foundations forming a variety of rectangular shapes.

This collection of remains, puzzling to the expert and completely baffling to the uninitiated, is the theatre of Dionysus as it was laid bare by excavation in the nineteenth century. Nothing could illustrate better the difficulty of using archaeological evidence for the history of drama. Unlike the splendid theatre at Epidaurus (Plate 1b), which was the creation of a single architect and underwent few later modifications, the theatre at Athens passed through phase after phase of development and change. What we see today is the cumulative result of all

1a The Theatre of Dionysus at Athens

1b The Theatre at Epidaurus

2a Comic Actor on Platform

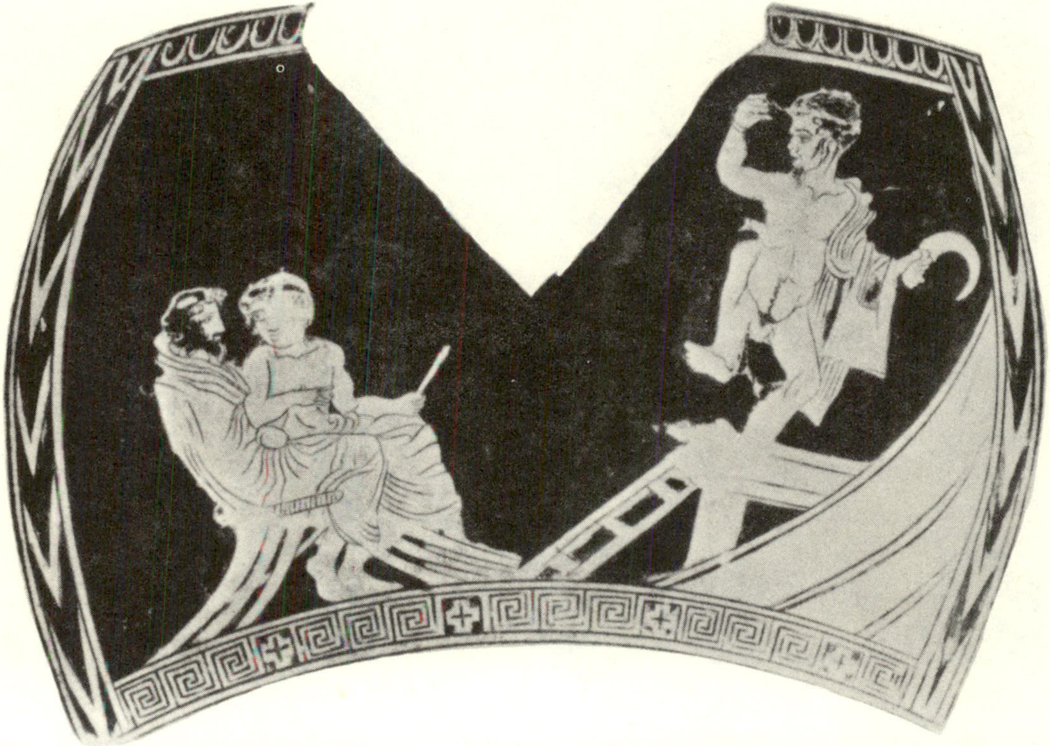

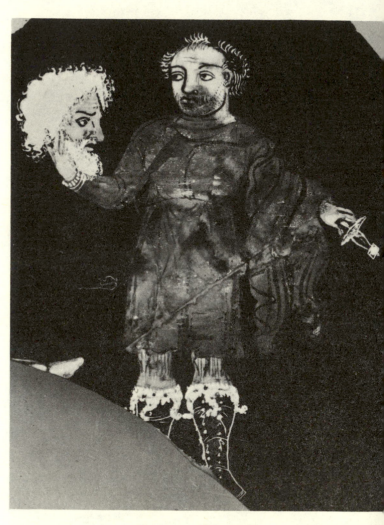

2b Actor with Mask

3   Actor from the Pronomos Vase

4 Chorus Men

the phases, but above all the product of the last—the alterations made by the Romans in the first three centuries A.D. when gladiatorial contests and perhaps even mock sea-fights were held where Aeschylus' chorus had once sung and danced. Of the theatre in those earlier days these relics from seven or eight hundred years later can tell us little, though that little, as we shall see, is of the highest value. To provide a setting for the tragedies as they were originally performed we need an effort of imagination, guided not only by expert examination of the theatre site but by the available evidence of every kind.

The oldest remnants on the site are slight but significant. They include part of the foundations of a small temple, and a curving row of six stones which must be a fragment of the supporting wall for a flat terrace at the foot of the Acropolis slope. Both may go back to the sixth century B.C. Here we have all that is left of the two main features of the precinct in the first years of drama: the temple of the god, and the level space (Greek: *orchestra*, dancing-place) on which the chorus performed their dances. Somewhere, whether on the edge of this place or further off, there must have been a tent or hut for the changing of masks or costumes, as there often is for an open-air performance today. (The Greek for this was *skene*, Latin *scaena*, our word 'scene'.) No doubt some spectators stood on the terrace round about, but others on the slope; and here in the course of time wooden seats were put up, supported on stands.

How long this simple arrangement was kept we cannot tell: some of the plays of Aeschylus might be done with nothing more. But it is clear that during the fifth century great changes were made. Certainly before the performance of the *Oresteia* in 458 B.C., and probably earlier, the simple changing-hut *skene* was replaced by more substantial structures. A disastrous collapse of wooden stands, perhaps in the market-place rather than the theatre, led to the creation of a carefully made *theatron*, or 'watching-place', on the slope. (The Latin *auditorium* means a place for listening.) Later its ramp

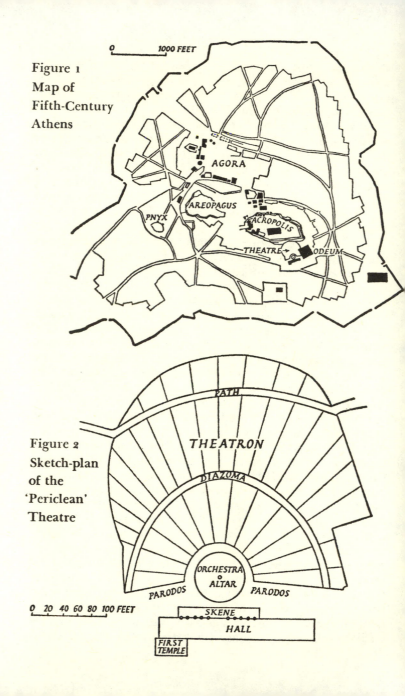

O   1000 FEET

Figure 1
Map of
Fifth-Century
Athens

AGORA

AREOPAGUS

PNYX

ACROPOLIS

THEATRE → ODEUM

Figure 2
Sketch-plan
of the
'Periclean'
Theatre

PATH

THEATRON

DIAZOMA

PARODOS   ORCHESTRA   o   ALTAR   PARODOS

0   20   40   60   80   100 FEET

SKENE

HALL

FIRST
TEMPLE

was made steeper and the dancing-circle was moved some yards nearer to the Acropolis. A second temple was erected to house a new gold and ivory statue of the god. For much of this reconstruction Pericles may have been responsible, although it can hardly have been completed in his lifetime; and it is this 'Periclean' theatre (Fig. 2) that needs closer examination as the setting for most of the tragedies we now possess. Consideration of it part by part must not obscure the fact that it was a unity—not as the work of one architect, but as an organic growth in which all the parts (and, as we shall see later, all the persons who filled them) were interconnected. In this theatre there was no proscenium arch or curtain to provide a barrier, no division into darkened auditorium and well-lit stage. Every part was open to every other under the open sky.

The auditorium is now unimpressive, and hardly suggests the huge crowd who sat there during the festivals. Most of the stone seating was removed in the Middle Ages and used for building materials elsewhere. Only the remains of retaining walls round the edge show the area that it once covered. In the Periclean theatre the seats of honour at the front may already have been made of stone; but all the rest of the spectators must have sat on backless wooden benches placed on rising terraces of earth. As description of the audience and their theatre-tickets has shown, they were divided into wedge-shaped blocks by narrow flights of steps. Some way up there was probably a level passageway from one side of the whole area to the other (Greek: *diazoma*, girdle); and near the top another way across was provided by an ancient path which ran along the Acropolis slope. Above this there were seats again, completing about eighty tiers in all; but whether this uppermost part was filled in the fifth century we cannot tell. The acoustics of the Periclean theatre with all its wooden seating cannot now be judged. They probably did not reach the perfection of the architect-planned auditorium at Epidaurus, where the tearing of a piece of paper in the dancing circle is audible on the back row. But even the comic poets never complain that actors or chorus could not be heard.

Of the *orchestra* which lay at the foot of the vast *theatron* there is now no trace as it existed in the fifth century B.C. Later versions superimposed have obliterated it completely, and we cannot be sure exactly where it was. That it was circular there can be little doubt, and it was about 60 feet across. The floor—if we may trust the analogy of Epidaurus—was of hard earth, not paved or covered; and in the centre stood a small stone altar of the god. Between this dancing-area and the front row of seats there was probably a gap several yards wide, and a drainage-channel must have run round the edge to take rainwater from the slope; but no barrier separated chorus and spectators like the marble slabs that in Roman times kept gladiators and audience apart. At either side were the passageways (Greek: *parodoi*) which were the spectators' main access to the auditorium before the plays began. By these the chorus normally reached the dancing-circle early in the play and left it at the end, and sometimes they provided entrances and exits for the actors as well. In later years, when for comedy at any rate the scene was normally Athens, a convention arose corresponding to what the audience could see from the theatre: as the Piraeus and the Agora lay to their right, entrance from harbour or market-place in the play must be by the *parodos* on that side; from open country, by the *parodos* on their left. But fifth-century tragedy usually explained each new arrival's identity and whence he came, as in Euripides' *Medea* (665–7):

MEDEA. Greetings to you, Aegeus, son of wise Pandion!
          Whence come you to visit this land of Corinth?
AEGEUS. I journey from Phoebus' ancient oracle.

Beyond these passageways, as we move away from the Acropolis, we come to the most substantial relics of the fifth-century theatre. The bottom part of a long straight wall two feet thick, which must have supported an extended terrace, stretches for 204 feet facing the auditorium, and from it a solid rectangle of stone built at the same time projects about nine feet towards the *orchestra*. Close against the other side of the wall are the remains of a long narrow hall which had an open colonnade and steps along most of the side away from the auditorium; and further south still are the foundations of the second temple. The purpose of the hall is disputed: its open side suggests some social use, such as shelter from rain, rather than a great store-room. But for the theatre as a setting for drama the most significant feature is to be found in the long wall opposite the dancing-circle. Vertical grooves or slots, originally ten in all, have been cut in the face of the stone on either side of the projecting rectangle. These grooves, with their suggestion of heavy wooden posts now lost, are our one important piece of material evidence for any structure in the acting area for the fifth-century plays.

These visible remains obviously leave open most of the questions to which we would like answers. What was the shape and size of the *skene* whose rear supports rested in the ten post-holes? How was the acting area related to the *orchestra*? On what level was it? Was there in any sense a stage? Was there scenery? What machinery and properties were used? To deal with these issues we have to turn to other kinds of evidence which all have their difficulties: to vase-paintings of doubtful relevance for the theatre, or at any rate for this theatre at this time; to the writings of Vitruvius and Pollux and other documentary sources which may be true of the theatre at various later dates, but have little value for the time of Pericles; most important of all, to the plays themselves, provided we can avoid preconceptions about how they were performed.

The post-holes for the back of the *skene* imply other supports further forward for its front; and most of the extant plays confirm that there was now a more elaborate structure overlooking the *orchestra* than the original tent or hut. If all the grooves were used it would be over a hundred feet long, but probably it was not more than twelve feet deep. Perhaps at either end it had projecting

41

wings (Greek: *paraskenia*) like the stone theatre buildings of later years, but this is a point on which there can
be no certainty. Evidently it was made of wood, and it
may well have been constructed afresh for each festival.
But such a substantial erection could hardly be put up
for single days, still less for particular plays: it must have
been there throughout the dramatic contest.

A wooden façade behind the actors would be an effective sounding-board for their voices, as well as setting off
their masks and colourful costumes; a great asset, in fact,
just as background to the performances. But the *skene*
had become more than this. Instead of a changing-tent
or hut, an external accessory like a dressing-room in the
modern theatre, it was now a place within the action of
the drama. It had become part of the make-believe, part
of the play, whether it stood in the audience's imagination for a palace or a temple or a general's tent or even
a cave. Characters in the play could be regarded as living
in it, and went in or came out. For the extant tragedies
only one door is essential, but it has been argued that
some of the comedies need at least two: probably by the
closing years of the fifth century there were three entrances in the façade, a great central one perhaps twelve
feet wide and smaller ones at either side.

Pollux writes of a *theologeion* above the *skene*—a
place from which the gods speak; and in some of the
plays of Aeschylus and Euripides it is clear that such a
higher level was required. The simplest explanation is
that in the fifth century at any rate it was provided by
the flat roof of the wooden structure itself, presumably
reached by stairs inside the building. No doubt its main
function was the one which the later name describes.
Aeschylus, for example, seems to have made use of it in
his *Weighing of Souls* (*Psychostasia*, now lost) for a remarkable scene in which Zeus weighed the destinies of
Achilles and Memnon while their divine mothers,
Thetis and Dawn, pleaded with him for their sons' lives.
For this celestial tableau the roof was imagined to be the
home of the gods, but it could also be treated as just the
roof of the palace, used by the solitary watchman of the

42

Agamemnon or by three human characters in the final episode of Euripides' *Orestes*.

The height of the *skene* is uncertain, though some have thought a scene in Euripides involved an actor's leap from roof to ground, and drawn the conclusion that it was no more than nine or ten feet. Elevation to greater heights above the normal acting level was achieved by the theatre crane, usually called *mechane* by the Greeks (Latin: *machina*, our word 'machine'). The powers of this remarkable piece of equipment cannot have been as great as some have thought: in Aeschylus' *Prometheus* it can scarcely have raised aloft the whole chorus of the Daughters of Oceanus in their winged car and held them in the air through 160 lines of the play. It may be doubted whether Aeschylus employed the crane at all, and there is no sign of it in Sophocles. But Euripides was notorious for ending his dramas with 'a god from the machine', and on occasion made more venturesome use of it: in the lost play called *Bellerophon* the hero was lifted skywards on his winged steed Pegasus (surely a dummy, not a live horse!). Unfortunately the details of the 'machine' are uncertain. We cannot be sure where it was situated. It appears to have had an arm which could be raised by means of ropes and pulleys, while the actor or his carriage or mount dangled from it in a harness attached to a hook. It is not surprising that Aristophanes saw the crane as a good subject for parody, or that the actor seems to have found his ride through the air a hazardous experience. The farmer-hero of the *Peace* flies heavenwards on a giant dung-beetle like Bellerophon on Pegasus, and shouts (174), 'Hi, crane-operator, take care of me!'

The actor could appear, then, on the *skene* roof, or be lifted even higher above it; but his normal place was the area in front of the wooden façade. These few square yards have become a scholars' battleground. Their relation to the dancing-circle has been the most controversial of all the many problems of the fifth-century theatre. Ancient writers on the Greek theatre assume that it had a stage some ten or twelve feet high. The absence of any archaeological evidence for the existence of this in the fifth century is not a conclusive argument against it: a stage, like the *skene,* could have been made of wood and disappeared without trace. More decisive are the requirements of the plays themselves for the intermingling of actors and chorus. It is true that the two had different functions which to a large extent kept them apart. But they are in too frequent contact to allow any great barrier like a ten-foot drop (or even a ten-foot staircase) between them. In several instances the chorus enter or leave through the *skene;* the actors come and go by the *parodoi* at the sides of the dancing-circle, and seem free to move anywhere between the *skene* and the front row of the audience as the action demands. Even without this definite evidence from the plays, an arrangement which put the actors on such a different level would scarcely be credible for the period when they were still a recent offshoot from the chorus. The high stage of the ancient commentators does not fit the Periclean theatre but belongs to a later time when the actors whom it lifted into prominence were all that mattered in the play.

Two alternatives remain. Either the normal acting area was the part of the dancing-circle furthest from the audience and any space between this and the *skene*: those who adopt this view allow that there may have been one or two broad steps at the base of the wooden façade on which the actor might occasionally stand, but for the most part place him on the same level as the chorus. The other possibility is to make him more easily visible to the spectators by putting him on a low platform, presumably of wood, communicating with the *orchestra* by a few steps or stairs. Sockets which may have held supports for such a platform are to be found in the remains of some other Greek theatres. Its appearance in comic scenes on fourth-century vases from Southern Italy proves nothing about Periclean Athens, but a much-discussed Attic vase-painting of about 420 B.C. (Plate 3a) may perhaps be more relevant. A comic actor burlesquing Perseus looks out from a low platform to which steps are attached, and at their foot are two seated

44

figures (poet and *choregos*, or symbolic audience?). There is no sign of a chorus or any place for them, and one may doubt whether the picture has any connection with the theatre of Dionysus. But if it has and there was a platform for the comedies, it must have been used for the tragedies as well. Comedy shared the same festival as tragedy; during the Peloponnesian War, even the same day.

The dimensions of this hypothetical wooden structure are of course conjectural, since we know neither the size of the *skene* building nor the precise position of the *orchestra*. Whatever its length, it probably had little depth unless it cut off a segment of the dancing-circle; to allow reasonable freedom of movement between the two levels, it could hardly have been more than three or four feet high. 'Platform' is a better word for it than 'stage', which suggests false analogies with the theatre of today. Whether we envisage the actor thus slightly elevated above the chorus or leave him on their level, lack of depth is the most striking feature of his main perform-ing area, and it was ill adapted for acting in the modern sense. The name later applied to it—*logeion*, speaking-place—is a significant contrast with the *orchestra*, the dancing-place of the chorus. The next chapter will discuss how much truth there is in the implication of the two terms that the function of the chorus was to dance; of the actor, to speak his lines.

On one level or another the actor performed his part near the *skene*, which was now a place involved in the play. But how far did this or anything else in the acting area provide scenery in the modern sense, a distinctive setting suited to a particular plot? About two-thirds of the extant tragedies take place in front of a palace or a temple; in others the action is on the sea-shore or among mountains or in a camp. In the group of tragedies and satyr-play which Euripides presented in 431 B.C. the scene altered from outside Medea's house to a desert island, then to a palace, and from there to country; if a comedy was performed in the afternoon, it brought still another move, to a street with two or three houses. Occasionally there is a change within a single play: in Aeschylus' *Eumenides*, from Apollo's temple at Delphi to the Areopagus at Athens; in Sophocles' *Ajax*, from a military camp to the sea-shore. How (if at all) were these various settings represented? The question is one of basic importance for our understanding of Greek tragedy. We are familiar with the use of more or less realistic scenery in the theatre and it is easy to assume that the Greeks must have used it too; but it will be better to put the assumption aside and look at the evidence.

Aristotle says in the *Poetics* (4) that Sophocles introduced *skenographia* into the theatre. The word is usually translated 'scene-painting', and taken to mean that 'sets' or 'backcloths' were made picturing the scene of each play, or at any rate of those set in a country or sea-shore landscape. To be visible to the vast audience, such backcloths would have to be large and bold. In a daylight performance without curtain or 'flies', scene-shifters would have to carry them on and off openly in front of the audience. (There is no suggestion, ancient or modern, that the crane was used to move them.) Sometimes, as we have seen, they would have to be changed in the middle of the play.

There is nothing here that cannot be paralleled in the modern theatre; but we have no need to postulate such practices in the theatre of Sophocles, for the most likely interpretation of *skenographia* is not 'scene-painting', but 'painting of the *skene*'—which could be a very different thing. An explanation of Aristotle's statement comes centuries later from Vitruvius (VII *praef.* 11), who tells us that it was Agatharchus who first 'made a *scaena*' at Athens, and goes on to imply that his innovation was the portrayal of architectural perspective. Vitruvius connects it with a performance of Aeschylus— probably a revival, since there are good reasons for dating it well after Aeschylus' death. From Aristotle and Vitruvius together one inference emerges; that sometime in the second half of the fifth century Agatharchus devised the art of painting an architectural design in perspective on the *skene* in front of which the actors moved. Nothing suggests that the design was intended to make the *skene* represent a particular kind of building: presumably it remained the same for all plays, at any rate through one festival.

There is no 'scenery' here in our normal sense of the word; nor is it to be found anywhere else in evidence relevant to the fifth century B.C. It is not in the *Poetics*: Aristotle makes several mentions of the visual aspect of drama (*opsis*), but what he has in mind is the appearance of the actors or chorus; 'spectacle', with its suggestion of scenic marvels, is a misleading translation of the Greek.[1] More remarkable still, scenery prompts no jokes in comedy: in Aristophanes, who has fun with the crane and other devices used in the performance of tragedy, there is no trace of satire on outrageous backcloths or hurrying sceneshifters, nor does any later commentator refer to anything of the kind in comedies now lost.

If we turn to art, we find nothing at this time to suggest the existence of any practice of scene-painting. The vase-painter concentrates on human beings and the human environment, and indicates natural surroundings by the simplest of symbols—a dolphin for the sea, blades of grass or a pair of bay trees for the land. Vase decoration is of course far removed from the work of an Agatharchus; but it is difficult to believe that in a period when a first-rate vase-painter pictured a Muse in her mountain haunt by seating her on a rock labelled 'Helikon', great landscape backcloths were in use in the theatre. Such evidence as we have for fifth-century wall-painting points to the same slight and symbolic treatment of nature as on vases. More than two centuries passed before large-scale landscape-painting came into its own.

If this line of thought is right, the fifth-century theatre

---

[1] An apparent exception is 1456a2, but *opsis* here is a doubtful emendation of the text; and its originator, Bywater, took the word even here as referring to the appearance of 'the strange personages introduced'.

knew nothing of 'scenery' as we understand it. What, then, of the plays and their variety of setting? We are driven to the conclusion that whether the characters were supposed to be outside a temple or palace or encampment or in the country or on the shore, all the action took place in front of the same façade with its door or doors, decorated perhaps with painting in perspective. It may well be that a simple wooden shape representing an altar or a tomb was sometimes placed at a little distance from the façade. Wooden statues of the gods, probably brightly coloured, are other likely theatre properties. Possibly light screens representing rocks could be brought on, if only to hide one character from another, but it is simpler to believe that Greek tragedy and its audience took for granted the same convention as Roman comedy—that a character can stay unseen and unheard by others as long as it suits the dramatist to keep him so. These are minor, though much debated, issues. The essential point is that where the modern theatre-goer looks for a 'set' designed to fit a particular play, his Athenian counterpart expected and found little or nothing more than a familiar structure used in all the plays. For the rest imagination, stimulated and guided by words, was enough. When the chorus of Euripides' *Ion* (206–7) admire a series of scenes from mythology on the temple-front—

> See, carved on the marble walls,
> The rout of the Giants by the Gods in battle!

—it is their words that enable the audience to share the sight, not a backcloth carried on at the beginning of the play. When Troy is set ablaze at the end of the *Trojan Women*, there was no spectacle such as modern stage mechanism and lighting can produce—nothing more than the cries of the chorus or Hecuba (1295–7):

> O horror, horror!
> Troy is aflame, the houses on the hill are burning,
> The city and the ramparts!

It was left to the Romans in Nero's time to burn a real house down on the stage.

In all this the Greek theatre may be at variance with our own; but it is in agreement with the practice of other times and cultures, including those in which drama has reached its greatest heights—Shakespeare's theatre, for example, with its unchanging background of doors, alcove and balcony; the Japanese Noh theatre, with its unvarying picture of a pine tree on the rear wall of the acting area; or Sanskrit drama, picturesque and exotic in the setting which its words convey, yet performed on a completely bare stage. In the history of world theatre as a whole freedom of imagination has been the rule: it is our own age, in so far as it is tied to visual realism, that is out of step.

To this free roving of the imagination there was one limit in the Greek fifth-century theatre, which differentiates it from the potentialities of a completely bare stage or the kaleidoscopic succession of different scenes in Elizabethan drama. The *skene* itself, whether it did duty for palace or temple or tent or cave, could and usually did provide a point of reference to which all the action of the play was related. Unity of place was no absolute rule, and it is not surprising that it is not mentioned by Aristotle in the *Poetics*, although Renaissance editors thought they found it there: in the course of a single play, as we have seen, the area in front of the façade could shift in imagination from Delphi to Athens, from camp to beach. Such freedom was greater in Aeschylus than his successors, especially Euripides. But the presence of the chorus gave all Greek drama a continuity which Shakespeare lacks, and in the majority of tragedies the imagined function of the *skene* and the space before it remained the same. Here all the visible action of the play took place—outside, in the open; a setting which may seen strange in colder climates, but was not unnatural for Greeks who spent much of their daily life in the open air. We have only to think of the Assembly listening to the speakers under the open sky, of Socrates talking in the streets or the market-place, or of the theatre itself.

Here was the single focal point of the play, one of the features that make Greek tragedy seem static, but give it a concentration beside which Shakespeare is often loose and fragmentary. To this point all the characters must come to take their part in the action. But it is a focus in a wider sense than this. The visible action performed here in front of the audience is far from embracing all the events of the play. Many of them, including the most violent, take place elsewhere, and instead of a change of scene to show the event itself, news of it is brought to this point by a messenger. The ancient Greeks were not squeamish about violence or death: from the *Iliad* onwards bloodshed was a commonplace in narrative poetry, as it was in vase-paintings and indeed in ordinary life. It is not true that death or physical suffering was never enacted in the theatre. Alcestis and Hippolytus die, Heracles and Oedipus are seen in agony, Prometheus has a stake driven through his chest. In the *Poetics* (11) Aristotle refers to 'deaths openly presented, great sufferings, woundings and the like' without any suggestion of a ban on such sights: some of the plays now lost may well have included them. Yet the fact remains that in the extant tragedies violence and murder normally occur 'offstage': there are no exciting duels, no bloodthirsty spectacles. Explanations have been sought in religious taboo, or in difficulties arising from the limitation of the number of actors; but whatever the origin of the practice, its retention reflects once more a readiness to trust imagination more than sight, the ear rather than the eye. In one of Plato's dialogues (*Ion* 535e) a professional reciter of Homer describes the effect of his performance on the audience. 'Whenever I look down at them from the platform,' he says, 'I see them weeping, gazing wildly at me, marvelling at what they hear.' A public accustomed to be so moved by recitation of the *Iliad* would find the agonies of the dying Heracles (in Sophocles' *Women of Trachis*) or the rending of Pentheus (in Euripides' *Bacchae*) far more vivid in the messenger's account than through any realism that the Greek style of acting could achieve. (How often, for that matter, is

murder on the stage convincing today?) What the
Athenian audience did expect to see was not violence
itself, but its sequel. In a climax prepared for by the
messenger's speech, the result of the reported action is
often brought to the same focal point before the *skene*
façade: Hippolytus is carried in to die; deluded queen
Agave marches triumphantly in holding her own son's
head.

We come back to the *skene* itself. How did its dramatic
function fit into the general picture? In many of the
extant tragedies a good deal of the action takes place
'within'; but the Greeks never developed the conception
of an interior scene made visible to the audience by the
stage convention which we take for granted—the removal
of one wall of a room. Perception of events behind the
skene façade was limited to what was heard, not seen,
and conveyed to the audience by the comments of characters outside or the chorus: Medea's cries of anger and
hatred at Jason's new marriage; the death-shrieks of
Clytemnestra; or—more subtle use of the same device—
Phaedra listening at the door as Hippolytus inside the
palace curses the nurse who has betrayed her secret.
Otherwise what occurred 'within' was treated in the
same way as what happened on the mountain or the sea-
shore or in some other distant place. It could be related
by a messenger (Greek: *exangelos*, one who carried news
out from inside the house); and its results could be
brought out in front of the audience. When Oedipus
discovers the appalling truth about his past he rushes
into the palace and the door is closed. A slave comes out
and tells how Jocasta has hanged herself and Oedipus
has destroyed his own sight. The audience has watched
the blinding in imagination through the messenger's
report. Now the door opens and the blinded king stands
before them.

The re-entry of Oedipus, blind as he was, presented
no difficulties; and in Sophocles' play the dead Jocasta
remained unseen. But it is clear that in some tragedies
the whole outcome of the catastrophe within was made
visible, including the dead. These scenes were not static

tableaux: they could involve speech and action, out of which flowed the further development of the play. In the *Agamemnon* of Aeschylus Clytemnestra is revealed beside the bodies of her husband and Cassandra, triumphantly holding the net in which the king has been entangled and glorying in his death. Near the end of the sequel, the *Libation-Bearers*, comes a significantly similar grouping—Orestes standing over the dead Clytemnestra and Aegisthus, with once more the fatal net: as he stands there he sees the avenging Furies approaching, and rushes off to seek refuge at Delphi. In the *Hippolytus* the door is opened at Theseus' command and the dead Phaedra is seen: tied to her wrist he finds a letter accusing his son, whom he curses and so brings to disaster. In *The Madness of Heracles* the opening of the door reveals Heracles asleep, bound to a broken pillar, with his wife and children lying dead in front of him: presently, like Agave, he comes to his senses and realises what he has done.

The way in which such scenes were managed is one of the most controversial issues in the history of the Greek theatre. Some have argued that the opening of the door and revelation within the doorway was enough; but there can be little doubt that the two leaves of the door opened *inward*, and a tableau arranged beforehand would have been some six feet behind the façade: the spectacle would have been scarcely visible in much of the auditorium, and words spoken scarcely audible either. It is better to accept the evidence, confused though it is, of later writers and commentators who say that even in the fifth century a special mechanism was used: the *ekkyklema*, or 'thing wheeled out'. Two versions of it have been inferred from their statements: one like an elementary form of the modern revolving stage; and a simpler device which seems more likely for the fifth century—a low wheeled platform (not larger, it has been calculated, than ten feet wide by six feet deep) which was pushed out through the central opening of the *skene*. If it is asked whether figures on this platform, words spoken from it, actions related to it, were inside or outside the palace, the answer must be that no such question troubled playwrights or spectators, any more than it worried Shakespeare in many of his scenes, or occurs to a modern audience watching a performance on an open stage. When the *ekkyklema* was in use the distinction between 'inside' and 'outside' was blurred until the poet needed to reassert it.

If this platform on wheels with its burden of horror seems comic today, it is interesting that the Athenians were also prepared to find it so. One of the strongest reasons for believing that it existed in the fifth century is that two passages of Aristophanes have little point unless they were making fun of it. In *Women at the Thesmophoria* (95) the tragic poet Agathon is 'wheeled out'; and when in the *Acharnians* (407–9) Euripides is too busy to come out of his house to see the farmer-hero, the latter shouts 'Be wheeled out, then!'—and so he is. On this as on other questions, comedy provides some of the best evidence for the presentation of tragedy. But in any case the *ekkyklema*, strange though it may seem to us, was a logical means to the achievement of the centripetal effect which this chapter has emphasised. No realistic scenery fettered the imagination of the audience, which was free to be carried by the magic of words to remote scenes of action or across vast distances of space and time; but the bringing of report and result to a single unchanging central point is one of the features that gave Attic tragedy at its best its unique concentration and intensity of impact.

6

The Performance

FROM the place we turn to what was done there on the days of the contest in tragedy; from the theatre to the performance. A play at the festival of Dionysus was a single indivisible occasion in which all present—actors, chorus, audience—shared in their different ways. The relationship that bound them together is an essential part of our picture; but to get the picture clear we must begin by trying to separate the inseparable and look at each of the three in turn.

First, the tragic actor. (Acting in comedy was regarded as a separate art.) In the earliest days of tragedy there was only one actor—the poet himself. Aristotle tells us in the *Poetics* (4) that Aeschylus increased the number to two, and Sophocles added a third. The author was no longer expected to act. Sophocles, we are told, gave it up because of the weakness of his voice, although he played the lyre in one of his plays and is said to have delighted the audience by playing ball in the part of Nausicaa. In 449 B.C. a prize was established for acting, and now the chief actor is named along with poet and *choregos* in inscriptions. So began the actors' profession, which within a few decades came to dominate the theatre.

Three things stand out in our information on this development. First, it is exclusively concerned with actors; there were no actresses, in spite of the outstanding women characters in the plays—Clytemnestra, Electra, Hecuba, Medea. The high status of the profession in itself made the idea unthinkable: only free and respectable women could have belonged to it, and no woman of this sort in Athens could be imagined performing in a public place. Nor were boys used to give a semblance of women's voices, as in the Elizabethan theatre. All female roles were taken by men.

54

The second striking feature is the all-important position of the chief actor, the protagonist, who inherited the place originally filled by the poet himself. Only he was said to 'act' the play, only he could win the acting prize. In the performance he was not so marked off from the rest as his counterpart the *shite* in the Noh plays of Japan, who alone dances and wears a mask and splendid costume. But his fellow-players the 'deuteragonist' and 'tritagonist' were expected to keep their place and never to steal the show. In the fourth century famous stars of the theatre could command huge fees and were used as ambassadors on missions of state.

The third point is the most remarkable. Once the number of speaking actors had reached three, there it remained. This does not mean, of course, that there could be only three characters in the play. Usually there were two or three times as many parts, which the actors divided between them; and in addition a number of non-speaking 'extras' which varied according to the generosity of the *choregos*: sometimes the acting area was a scene of pageantry. But very rarely, if ever, did it carry more than three speaking characters at once. How the parts were shared in particular plays we are not told, except for a few which were acted by famous protagonists. But scholars have tried to work the puzzle out, with some strange results. In Sophocles' *Antigone* the same actor is likely to have played both Antigone and Haemon: certainly the part of Ismene was combined with that of the Guard. In Euripides' *Bacchae* the deuteragonist probably 'doubled' king Pentheus and Agave, the king's mother who kills him. In his *Ion* and *Electra* one actor (presumably the tritagonist) carried four parts, in the *Orestes* at least five. In Sophocles' *Oedipus at Colonus* it seems simplest to suppose that one character, Theseus, was played by all three actors in turn; or perhaps here and in some cases where a child speaks a fourth was allowed.

It is clear that the playwrights sometimes found themselves in difficulties over this three-actor rule. It called for some lightning changes of mask and costume within the *skene* while a few lines were spoken outside. It caused some strange and improbable silences. At the end of the *Orestes* Euripides attempted a *tour de force* with a scene which brought six or seven of the ten characters at one time before the audience, but at least three of them, including Orestes' friend Pylades, were necessarily represented by silent 'extras'. When Orestes is about to kill Hermione and Menelaus asks Pylades whether he shares in the murder, the playwright solves his difficulty by making Orestes reply (1592):

> His silence gives consent; my word will be enough.

Why was a rule sometimes so inconvenient retained? If Aristotle's account of the rise to three actors is correct, there was no religious reason. Partial explanations can be found in the need for all poets competing in the contest to be restricted to the same number, or in the difficulty of finding enough actors for all the plays at the festival. But it is significant that in the extant tragedies even the three actors available are seldom fully used. Most scenes consist largely of duologue, and three characters rarely talk for long together. Evidently the rule persisted because the playwrights had no great desire to break it, no strong inclination (in spite of the final scene of the *Orestes*) towards complicated situations or cross-talk. Their use of the actors reminds one of the acting area with its single focal point: here again the aim was not complexity but simplicity, not diffusion and dissipation of effect but concentrated intensity, which the dominance of the protagonist still further strengthened.

We are dealing, then, with three actors, to whom a number of 'extras' could be added. What did they look like? How did they move and speak? What did acting a part mean?

The tragic actor of antiquity is often visualised as a horrific figure with elongated forehead, staring eyes, gaping mouth, long sweeping robe and thick-soled boots raising him several inches off the ground. This grim statuesque shape with its foreboding of untold horror and inevitable doom has coloured our whole conception of Greek tragedy, but it did not exist in the time of Sophocles. The picture was derived from the art of later centuries when the earlier costume had been distorted into this form, and from Pollux and other late writers whose descriptions were imagined to be true of the fifth century B.C. Today it is recognised that our only reliable evidence for this period is the relevant remains from contemporary or near-contemporary art, including some discovered in recent years, in conjunction with occasional inferences from the plays themselves. Even here, as we have seen, there is great uncertainty: how far was a vase-painter guided by the realities of theatre practice, how far by imagination? Nevertheless, we can arrive at a rough idea of the actor as he must have appeared when the extant tragedies were first performed.

First, the mask, the part of his costume which seems strangest to us. It was made of linen, or occasionally of cork or wood; this is why none have survived, except marble or terracotta copies made for some purpose such as dedication to a god. The mask covered the whole head or most of it and had hair attached: no separate wigs were used. The face, probably painted white or off-white for women and darker for men, had natural features boldly drawn, with small holes in the eyes for the actor to see through and slightly open mouth. Pollux lists twenty-eight stock masks for tragic characters; how much division into types there was in the fifth century, if any, we do not know. Occasionally (if visual realism went so far) an actor representing the same character may have changed to a second mask: Oedipus, for example, when he comes out from the palace with blood streaming from his now sightless eyes.

Why did the actors wear masks? In many parts of the world they are or have been used in ritual, and masked figures in Greek art long before the supposed beginnings of drama point to a religious or magical origin. On the other hand tradition told that Thespis, the creator of tragedy, at first used white lead make-up and only later took to masks. Whatever the route by which their use came into drama, masks were retained and taken for granted by the Greeks through the centuries because in the Greek theatre they were right: they were the logical means to a required end. In the comparatively small theatres of modern times facial expression is all-important for the actor, and he leaves his face uncovered though he may disguise it with make-up: a smile or a frown may mean more to the audience than anything said. But actors at Athens were at least twenty yards from the spectators in the front row on the other side of the *orchestra*, nearly a hundred yards from the back of the auditorium. At such distances change of face was hardly visible, and even if there had been no masks the same practice of describing the characters' expression would have been necessary which we find in the plays. In Euripides' *Medea*, for example (922-3):

> Jason (*to Medea*): What is this? Why these tears that wet your eyes?
> Why are you pale? Why do you turn away?

What mattered to the Greek audience, who had no programmes to guide them, was the same need for quick identification which was often met by naming a new arrival on the scene. Given some knowledge of the story, they could tell immediately from the actor's mask which character in it was before them. Most important of all, masks alone made it possible for the actor to *change* identity, so that the spectators who had watched him as Aphrodite could accept him a little later as Phaedra, and later again as Theseus.

Character-drawing, of course, was the loser by the use of masks (or perhaps we should say, by the size of the Greek theatre): the mask could surpass the face in idealising a character, but nothing more. The painter of a fourth-century mixing-bowl from Tarentum (Plate 2b) brings out the contrast between the idealised fair-haired mask and the elderly actor who holds it, with his stubbly beard and receding hair. But what subtleties of character could that face convey if the unchanging mask did not hide it! As we shall see later, such portrayal of character as existed in Greek tragedy was done by other means.

For the rest of the fifth-century actor's apparel we turn again to vase-paintings, but with less confidence. When the painter shows a figure wearing or holding a mask or accompanied by a flute-player, this can be taken as evidence for what the actor wore; but a figure apparently in special robes may or may not be relevant to the theatre. It is clear, however, that the Greeks had no idea of 'period' costume, attempting realistic reproduction of the past; and because they had no conception of this, its opposite did not enter into their thinking—the idea of doing a play in 'modern dress'. What influences shaped the actor's appearance we do not know—whether Eastern origins, or ritual garments worn in the worship of Dionysus or other gods. But what emerged by the time of Pericles seems to have been what the theatre required: a splendid and striking adaptation of contemporary dress specially suited to the actor's needs. Because he must catch the eye from a distance, his costume was richly decorated with an arresting pattern, and we may guess that often it was brilliant in colour, though black was worn by characters in mourning. Because even in one play he must be able to take a variety of parts, female as well as male, his own physical identity was completely concealed: mask, costume and footwear together covered him entirely except for his hands. His robe was usually ankle-length (not always, as Plate 2b shows). Unlike the normal dress of the time, it had long sleeves which hid his too obviously masculine arms. On his feet he seems to have worn soft thin-soled boots, sometimes decorated and laced, which reached some distance up the calf of the leg. Plate 3 illustrates the tragic actor's appearance from our most striking piece of evidence—a late fifth-century mixing bowl bearing figures whose costume must be near to that of tragedy, although the painter is portraying preparations for a satyr-play.

What has been described so far was the general type. There is little evidence to show how far variations were

made from it to distinguish individual actors—the protagonist and his inferiors; or different characters—young
and old, master and slave, even man and woman or
divine and human. Much may have been done with
simple properties: Apollo's bow, Heracles' club and lion-
skin; a sceptre for a king, a sword for a warrior, a wreath
for a herald. But any differentiation was likely to be of
this symbolic sort rather than on realistic lines. In a
play of Euripides now lost, king Telephus disguised himself as a beggar: Aristophanes repeatedly ridicules the
poet for making him appear in rags.

Such headgear, costume, footwear would not impede
the actor greatly or turn him into a figure so stiff and
statuesque as his horrific counterpart in later centuries.
But the question of the nature of his movements is one
of the worst gaps in our knowledge of the fifth-century
theatre. The plays often call for rapid motion or strong
gesture: characters are said to embrace or kneel or beat
the breast or throw themselves on the ground. We have
no information as to how the moves to fit these situations
were planned or carried out. The chorus, as we have
seen, were instructed and drilled, originally by the poet
himself, later by a professional trainer. The actors also
must have been under the poet's direction as long as he
was one of them, but when the chief part came to be
taken by a professional actor it seems probable that this
protagonist must have been 'producer' for them all; how
they were 'produced', what kind of direction they were
given, we do not know. On the whole it seems likely
that compared with modern realism all Greek acting
tended to be formal and stylised. A passage in the *Poetics*
(26) refers to controversy between actors in the fifth
century over styles of acting: Mynniscus, the protagonist
in some of Aeschylus' later plays, called a younger actor
an 'ape' because he overacted; and this meant, as the
context shows, because he was always on the move. The
story fits in with several features of the theatre and the
plays which point to a type of acting much simpler and
less realistic than today. One, as we have seen, is the lack
of depth in the acting area; another is the avoidance of

violence; a third, the patterned structure of the dialogue, of which more will be said in the next chapter. Most important of all, there was the predominance of the voice and the spoken word.

We have been looking at the actor as a striking, though distant, spectacle for the eye. But above all he was a voice, reaching out over the *orchestra* to the most remote rows of the vast auditorium. We are uncertain of the actor's appearance and know little or nothing of his moves and gestures; but there is ample evidence to show that it was his voice that mattered most. This was his greatest asset, which qualified him to become an actor and determined his prospects in the profession. To improve it he would go through meticulous training, fasting and dieting and seizing every chance of rehearsing. Strength of voice was the first essential, so that it could be heard throughout the theatre without shouting: there is no reason to suppose, as was once thought, that the mask did anything to enlarge it. But other qualities were equally necessary: clarity, correctness of diction (the comic playwrights never tired of making fun of one notorious mispronunciation), fineness of tone, adaptability to character and mood. The Greek actor had to be able to change his voice, as well as his mask, from young to old or from man to woman. He had to show the same versatility in utterance as a modern actor displays in facial expression. He must be equally effective in argument and narrative, the two uses of the spoken word which counted most in the theatre, as in the public life of the city as a whole. But not only speech was required of him. He must also have a knowledge of music and be expert in recitative, chanting in various rhythms to a flute accompaniment; and sometimes in moments of high emotion he must break into song, whether a lyric solo or stanzas sung in alternation with the chorus. It is not surprising that men with such talents were in short supply, though the resultant limitation to three actors, as has been said, suited the poets well enough. Nor is it strange that references to actors in Greek literature usually read like comments on opera singers. For the actor, as for the opera singer, the voice must have come first: looks, movement, gesture, important as they were, took second place.

From the actors we turn to the chorus. In modern productions of Greek tragedy they are often no more than a nuisance, getting in the way of the actors in the dialogue scenes or reciting obscure odes, not quite in unison, while the audience waits for the play to start moving again. In ancient times also they came to be regarded as an irrelevant and unnecessary interruption: as early as the begining of the fourth century Agathon began the practice of writing choral interludes which would do as well in one play as another. But in our extant tragedies such irrelevance is rare; and although the importance of the chorus for the plot declined and the proportion of the play given to them shrank, we may be sure that all through the fifth century it was an integral part of the performance, which no less than the actors made its contribution to the occasion as a whole.

The chorus also wore masks and a variable costume. A fifth-century vase now in Boston (Plate 4) shows two young men who are part of a female chorus. One is dressing, with his mask on the ground in front of him; the other, already dressed, seems to be rehearsing his part. In this painting masks and clothes are simple, and probably chorus costume in general lacked the splendour of the actors. But a few decades later figures on an Attic mixing-bowl include other members of a female chorus in highly decorated robes. It is clear from the plays that the look of the chorus differed with their imagined age or sex, nationality or occupation. One common type, old men, would carry a staff; another, women in mourning, would dress in black with the hair on their masks cut short. Others were more exotic: the daughters of Danaus, newly arrived from Egypt 'in foreign robes and headgear'; the Bacchae with their fawnskins and ivy-covered wands; the Furies with snakes in their hair. But an essential feature of the tragic chorus is that the costume was the same for the whole number—fifteen in the second half of the fifth century, perhaps twelve earlier, though some hold that Aeschylus sometimes used fifty. It is true that one of them was the leader, with a different function from the rest; and occasionally (not so often as some translators would have us believe) they spoke or chanted as individuals, or sang as two separate groups. But essentially they were a unity, well drilled to speak and sing and dance as one, their identical masks obliterating that most individual and variable part of the human body—the face.

For their movements contemporary art gives us little help, and we are dependent once more on Pollux and other late authorities, together with more or less doubtful inferences from the plays. When they first entered, usually after an opening scene or speech, they were preceded by their accompanist the flute-player—the only unmasked figure to come before the audience, who took up his position by the altar in the centre of the *orchestra*. The chorus themselves, we are told, marched in, and certainly in many plays their first lines are in marching rhythm (anapaests). Usually they were in three files of five each; but clearly neither this nor the marching was a strict rule, for the pursuing Fury chorus of the *Eumenides* (458 B.C.) and the searching old men of *Oedipus at Colonus* (produced 401 B.C.) entered in scattered groups or one by one, and in the *Prometheus* Aeschylus somehow brought in his chorus of Ocean-nymphs in a winged car. One thing is certain: having arrived, they stayed—with rare exceptions where departure and re-entry were necessary—till they marched off singing a few more lines of anapaests at the end.

What was their function through the play? In the *Poetics* (18) Aristotle opposes the irrelevance of the chorus in his own day by saying that it should be regarded as one of the actors (one, be it noted, not fifteen) and should take a share in the action. So it does in the extant tragedies, in varying degree. In Aeschylus' *Suppliants* the chorus is even at the centre of the plot, and its fate is the main issue at stake. Masks and costume are evidence that in all the plays the tragic chorus, unlike the dithyramb choruses earlier in the festival, had a dramatic role which linked it with the actors. Contact during spoken dialogue was through its leader, who in most of the plays has many lines to say, although he makes no long speeches. In the days of a single actor —the poet—talk between him and the chorus leader had been all the dialogue; hence the use of *hypokrites*, 'answerer', as the usual word for an actor. When the number of actors increased and they could be independent of the chorus, they still maintained their link with its leader, usually addressing him first when they came on the scene, replying to his questions, allaying his fears, waiting at the end of a speech for his expected and all too obvious two-line comment. In the later extant plays the leader's part declines, but other more effective patterns of contact increase: above all, passages of song (Greek: *kommos*) when the tension of the play rises to a climax of grief or horror or joy and one or more of the actors and the whole chorus give voice to their emotion in turn—the interchange between Sophocles' chorus and Oedipus when he re-enters with blinded eyes, or between Euripides' chorus and Electra and Orestes after the murder of Clytemnestra within the house.

What (if anything) did the chorus as a whole do during the spoken dialogue scenes, which generally constitute something like three-quarters of the play? The simple and safe reply is that we do not know, and probably never shall. But if we are considering the tragedies from the point of view of theatrical presentation it is important to inquire, even on speculative lines, where the major part of the cast were and what they did during the major part of the performance.

The traditional answer, based on a few late references which have to do with comedy, is that throughout the dialogue scenes the chorus maintained their three-row formation, facing towards the actors with their backs towards the spectators, and turning round only for the performance of their choral odes. This is perhaps credible for the later days of the high stage, if (as seems likely) the actors then performed on the stage and the chorus remained on the *orchestra* below. The chorus would not then have blocked the spectators' view of actors raised so high above them: they could even have been dramatically effective as a crowd watching and listening to the actors, enhancing the central import-ance of the action up on the stage. Such a picture accords well with the description of them by the writer of a passage in *Problems* (19, 48), a work attributed to Aris-totle but certainly compiled at a much later date: the chorus, he says, 'is an inactive watcher of events; for its only function is to display a friendly attitude to those who are on the stage at the same time'.[1] Of the Hellenis-tic theatre this may be true enough; but it is difficult to believe that in the fifth century B.C. the audience through most of the play was confronted with a tidy rectangle of immobile backs. The actors, on the same level as the *orchestra* or raised little above it, would have been partly invisible to the front rows—the most important rows—of the audience; and such complete passivity would surely have been out of keeping with the active role which the *Poetics* (unlike *Problems*) advocates for the chorus. We are driven to the conclusion that for the fifth century B.C. the traditional picture will not do.

On what we should put in its place we have little more than common sense to guide us. The chorus are un-likely to have behaved like a crowd in a modern pro-duction, showing individual feelings or pretending to talk among themselves; but as a body they surely must have reacted to what was said and done, and for their reactions to be visible they must have faced, or partly faced, the auditorium. Perhaps we should go farther, and put some trust in the muddled references made by scholiasts to some kind of 'dancing' by the chorus while the actors spoke. Is it possible that while the plot

[1] Translated by W. S. Hett in the Loeb Classical Library (New York, Harvard University Press; London, Heinemann).

developed and the actors' voices reached out over the auditorium, the chorus enriched the spectacle and gave a lead to the audience by 'dancing' the dialogue scenes, not with the synchronistic movement of the choral odes, nor necessarily with steps that took them from their places (we are familiar enough nowadays with the notion of dancing while remaining on the same spot), but with the rhythmic motions of hand and foot and head which were a great part of Greek dancing? Much of their movement may have been imitative miming, to which Plato and Aristotle often refer. How realistic it was, we cannot tell; but we may guess that their 'dancing' was the sort of physical reaction to the play which the audience might have shown if they had risen from their seats.

Whatever the truth on this difficult point, the function of the chorus even during the dialogue scenes was clearly more complex and subtle than Aristotle's claim that they should be like an actor suggests. Partly they resembled the actors and like them were inside the play. But they were also separated from the actors by differences apparent at every level: they were provided by the *choregos*, the actors by the state; they were 'produced' by the chorus-trainer, the actors probably by the protagonist; their place was the *orchestra*, the actors' area by the *skene*; they must last through to the end, whatever the actors' fate. From the historical point of view we have here two elements brought together at the creation of drama but never fully reconciled, with anomalous results which became less tolerable as realism in the theatre increased: the failure to intervene, variously excused, when cries for help come from the palace; the sharing of secrets with fifteen inconvenient eavesdroppers, who must be sworn to silence. It was inevitable that in time the chorus should cease to be thus both inside and outside the play, and Agathon's interludes placed it outside. But its dual function was part of the essence of tragedy as it existed in the fifth century, a cement which bound together the whole performance. From its place in the *orchestra* the chorus was linked on the one side with the actors, on the other

66

with the audience, who in these humble old men or attendant women watched people more like themselves than the heroic figures of the actors, and because of their own familiarity with choral dancing in the dithyramb contests and elsewhere felt through the movements of the chorus the rise and fall of the rhythm of the play.

The chorus are usually most 'outside the play' during the choral odes, those lengthy song systems which modern producers of Greek tragedy shorten, translators simplify, and readers are tempted to skip. Antigone has been led away to her death. Creon is silent. The chorus of old men sing the story of three others famous in legend who suffered the same fate as Antigone (944):

> Such was the fate, my child, of Danae
> Locked in a brazen bower,
> A prison secret as a tomb,
> Where was no day. . . .[1]

Their song, divided into two pairs of corresponding stanzas, combines metrical patterns to form a complex whole which is new and unique. So much is clear from the text; but of what all this meant in performance we know little. Of the music the main thing that can be said is that till late in the fifth century, at any rate, it did not distort or obscure the words. The poet was his own composer: he did not 'set words to music', but created for the chorus a song in which the music matched the quantitative rhythm of the words. The flute-player's function was an accompaniment, and no more. The singing was in unison: harmony in the modern sense of the term was unknown. The same correspondence with word-rhythm must also have been true of the dancing of the chorus, and metrical study of the odes enables us to judge whether the dance movements they involved were slow or fast, stately or excited. But beyond these generalities our ignorance is nearly complete. An ancient commentator states that while singing the first

[1] Sophocles, *Antigone*, translated by E. F. Watling (Penguin Classics).

of a pair of stanzas the chorus moved to the right (hence its Greek name: *strophe,* turning) and during its counterpart (Greek: *antistrophe*) they moved back; while if a single stanza or 'epode' was added, they stood still. Even if this is true, it tells us nothing of the miming moves and gestures, the physical expression of emotion and imagery which in the odes, if not during the dialogue, must have been the essence of the dance.

Out of words, music and dance together the poets and chorus-trainers created complicated patterns of sound and spectacle of a kind far removed from modern experience—the highest products of that tendency towards formal structure which runs all through Greek tragedy. For the audience at Athens they were exciting in themselves as masterpieces of craftsmanship: much of the argument about them in Aristophanes' *Frogs* turns on technical points. But what did these odes do for the play as a whole?

They have been compared with Shakespeare's comic scenes as means of brief escape from the otherwise unbearable pressure of the drama. Where Shakespeare brings his audience down to the earthy humour of the porter or the grave-digger, the Greek poet lifts their thoughts up onto the universal plane of their common mythology and common religious tradition—a region where the modern reader is easily bewildered and lost. The particular event is set in a wider perspective, feelings roused by the action of the preceding scene are calmed for the moment in a reflective pause. But it must not be thought that for the Greek audience the chorus divided or fragmented the play, as a modern production is broken by intervals filled with irrelevant chatter or visits to the bar. For the fifth-century Athenian, though not for his posterity in later times, tragedy remained an expansion of the still flourishing art of choral song, enclosed within its unifying choral framework. Although choral odes could cover an imaginary lapse of time, the drama was held together in a concentrated unity of action by the continuing presence of the chorus; and not only by their presence, but by the continuing spectacle of choral movement which must have reflected every change of situation or mood through all parts of the play.

We return to the audience, whose size and composition have already been discussed in describing the festival. How did they behave? What were their reactions to tragedy? What part did they play in the occasion as a whole?

It would be foolish to generalise. The performance they witnessed must have meant a variety of things to such a variety of people—Greeks from other states as well as Athenians; citizens and non-citizens of all classes and incomes; women and boys as well as men; even slave as well as free. Aristotle, for whom such distinctions are part of the natural order, contrasts two kinds of spectator in the theatre—the educated gentleman and the vulgar type drawn from mechanics and labourers and the like (*Politics* VIII, 7). Theophrastus in his *Characters* (11, 14) gives us thumbnail portraits of some individuals among the throng: the Boor, who hisses when everyone else is applauding and claps when everyone else is silent; the Blockhead, who goes to sleep during the show and is left still sleeping in the empty theatre at the end.

No doubt some slept, and others paid little attention to the performance. But for the most part, in different ways and on different levels, they were a critical audience. Not only the ten chosen men but all sat in judgment. This was a contest rousing all the emotions of partisanship; a contest, moreover, in which to the great mass of the audience the competitors were familiar—the poets, the *choregoi*, the actors, the choruses, whose members could well include a relative or a friend or a neighbour from the next street. Any play of Aristophanes, with its satire on Euripides or its gibes at a blundering actor or stingy *choregos*, is proof of the lively critical atmosphere on the benches at the festival.

Hostility or approval was not only felt, but expressed.

Although Dionysus' precinct was holy ground and all present were taking part in a common act of ritual, no solemn hush prevailed such as we now expect (in northern countries, at any rate) for great drama. There is no evidence for an organised claque till much later, but plenty for unorganised noise from the audience—clapping, shouting, hissing, drumming with the heels against the seats. Some spectators, Aristotle tells us (*Ethics* X, 5), created a disturbance when the acting was bad by noisily eating refreshments. It is not surprising that Plato (*Laws* 659a) talks disapprovingly of the judges being influenced 'by the uproar of the crowd'. We read, though mostly in connection with comedy, of the audience taking things into their own hands and hissing a play off, or pelting the actors with olives or figs or even stones. From Aristophanes and from stories (not always credible) in later writers we can gather what specially roused ire or approval. 'For what should one admire a poet?' asks Aeschylus in the *Frogs* (1008). 'For skill and good advice,' replies Euripides. Technical skill or blundering by author, actors or chorus was certainly one thing that the audience watched with critical eye or ear. They reacted still more strongly to 'advice' which they agreed with or found outrageous. Shouts of 'encore' (Greek: *authis*) might be raised if some lines took their fancy. On the other hand Seneca (*Epistle* 115) tells how their anger at a passage in praise of money would have brought a play of Euripides to a stop, if the poet himself had not rushed forward and begged them to see what happened to the character who uttered it. Speeches or odes in praise of Athens were an easy way for the playwright to gain applause. Nothing here points to a high general level of literary taste or dramatic criticism. Yet the fact remains that the popular favourites were the great tragic poets; above all, Sophocles, who rarely if ever seems to write just to please the crowd.

All this is concerned with the audience as critic, sitting in judgment on the play from outside. At a performance of tragedy they were always in a sense 'outside': there was none of the direct 'audience participation' which we find in fifth-century comedy, where the chorus harangued the spectators on topics of the day and the actors joked with them or even threw them figs and sweets. The tragic protagonist was not called on to anticipate a recent Shakespearian production in the United States, in which Hamlet left the stage and sold peanuts in the auditorium (London *Times* 21 January 1968). But an audience can be deeply involved in a play without any such direct contact with the players. We come here to a difficult question. When tragedy arose out of choral song, the essence of the change was an introduction of make-believe, of let's pretend. At the festival of Dionysus the Athenian audience made the same transition overnight, passing from the contest of unmasked dithyrambic choruses to the masked actors and chorus of drama. What was the difference between their attitudes on the one day and the next? In what way did they now become involved in make-believe, in illusion?

Obviously not in the same way as the audience in a modern proscenium-arch theatre, faced with realistic imitation of life in a realistic 'set'. The presence of the chorus was a fatal obstacle to such realism, and the necessary scenery and 'period' costumes were lacking. But make-believe need not depend on realistic visual aids. Symbols, well understood, can be enough, and so can words written by a great poet and spoken by a great actor, especially when they tell of things already partly known to the audience. Aeschylus' *Agamemnon*, originally performed at dawn on a spring morning in 458 B.C., opens with a watchman. The audience know him from the *Odyssey* (IV 524), but there he was stationed by Aegisthus on a rock by the sea to watch for the Greek fleet's return. Aeschylus has brought him within the compass of the theatre-setting by placing him on the roof of the palace at Argos, which the *skene* for the moment represents. He speaks:

O gods! grant me release from the long weary watch.
Release, O gods! Twelve full months now, night after night

> Dog-like I lie here, keeping guard from this high roof
> On Atreus' palace. The nightly conference of stars,
> Resplendent rulers, bringing heat and cold in turn,
> Studding the sky with beauty—I know them all. . . .[1]

Although the audience are sitting in the light, they accept in imagination that it is dark, just as Shakespeare's audience does in *The Merchant of Venice*:

> The moon shines bright: in such a night as this,
> When the sweet wind did gently kiss the trees
> And they did make no noise, in such a night. . . .

This is the magic of the theatre, achieved on the slopes of the Acropolis or in the Globe not by any scenic realism or trick of lighting, but by the spoken word. Whether we call it illusion or not, as Aeschylus' play went on it meant deep emotional involvement for the audience: Aristotle had good reason to talk of tragedy's power to arouse pity and fear. But involvement through poetry is a different thing from acceptance of an imitation of real life, and the two must not be confused. Scholars thinking in terms of realistic theatre have re-interpreted several of our extant Greek tragedies to explain away inconsistencies which they found incredible: in the *Oresteia*, for example, the arrival at Argos of a herald and then Agamemnon from Troy only a few hundred lines after the beacon signal has brought news of the city's fall; in Euripides' *Bacchae*, the fact that the palace is shattered in one scene, yet characters entering later behave as though it were unharmed. The explanations put forward for these 'impossibilities' are ingenious, but unnecessary. When roused and guided by the spoken word the imagination has a freedom of movement which it lacks when confined by the restrictions of realism—an ability to leap ahead through time, or to forget the past in order to concentrate on the present. It has no difficulty in passing quickly from Troy's fall to Agamemnon's grim homecoming, though

[1] Translated by Philip Vellacott in Penguin Classics.

in reality they must have been weeks or months apart. It sets aside the collapse of the palace (there is no debris, no broken masonry to keep it before us) and moves on to what happens next.

'The theatre was an empty shell,' writes Mr Peter Arnott in his book on *Greek Scenic Conventions* (p. 108), 'into which the dramatist could pour his ideas, setting the scene with his words and transcending all limitations of place and time.' He rightly adds that Aeschylus went furthest in exploiting the free imagination of the audience: in Euripides the restrictions of the beginning of realism are already closing in. But if the account of the performance of tragedy given in this chapter is correct, this is not the whole picture. Drama can take many forms, each with its own way of using the theatre and involving the audience; and the form which arose in Attica and became Greek tragedy is not simply to be put alongside others which have treated the theatre as an 'empty shell'. It was a unique development better suited to the Greek genius, embodying that combination of freedom and restraint which is typical of fifth-century Greek art. Aristotle was right in seeing unity as an essential feature of tragedy as he knew it. Its appeal was to the free imagination of the spectator, but its characteristic tendency was to concentrate that imagination on a single target. Later we shall see what this tendency meant in terms of treatment of plot. In this and the previous chapter we have been concerned with its manifestation in the performance of the play: the treatment of the area in front of *skene* as the single focal point to which the characters come, events elsewhere are reported, and their results are brought; the use of only three actors, with the protagonist as the chief centre of attention; most important of all, the chorus, which had not a dividing but a unifying effect, holding the action within a single framework and linking actors and audience in a single experience.

7

The Plays

WE come back to our primary evidence: the surviving plays. No attempt will be made here to describe or summarise them all, which would be a dreary substitute for reading them. The object of this chapter is to see how the tragic poet approached his task and created drama fitted to the occasion, the place, the style of performance which have been described: how he selected his material, from history or from legend; how he adapted it for presentation in the theatre, moulded it into a certain pattern; how he handled his characters; what part religious or philosophical thought played in his work. Particular plays (not always the best) will be used for illustration. Up to a point 'Greek tragedy' will be treated as a single type, but at this stage some differentiation between the three great tragic poets becomes inevitable.

Theatre audiences, it has been said, get the plays they deserve. Certainly the plays performed at the festivals of Dionysus were appropriate to the audience and the occasion, drawing their material from the common experience and common knowledge of the thousands who watched them—narrow limits compared with the extraordinary multiplicity of information available to modern man. Their subject-matter may seem remote and strange to us; but for the fifth-century Greeks massed at the festival their themes were common property shared by playwrights, performers, and audience alike. The point is most obvious for comedy, with its topical jokes and its caricature of the personalities of the day. Aristophanes held up a mirror—admittedly, a distorting mirror—to the present. The tragic poets, on the other hand, were concerned with the past, not as we now know it, but as it was seen by the community for which they wrote.

In the early decades of the century immediate past history was sometimes dramatised, evidently with a powerful impact on the audience. In 494 B.C. the city of Miletus, leader of the eastern Greeks in revolt against Persia, was besieged and stormed by the enemy: the men were killed, the women and children enslaved. Athens had failed to help. A year or two later the poet Phrynichus dramatised the disaster in a play called *The Capture of Miletus*. Its reception is reported by Herodotus (IV, 21):

> The whole audience burst into tears; and they fined him a thousand drachmas for reminding them of their own misfortunes, and decreed that no one should ever present that play again.

The first banned play, it appears, was prohibited because it touched too nearly the consciences of the audience. On the other hand the only surviving play on a theme from recent history is concerned with a Greek victory. Aeschylus' *Persians*, the earliest tragedy now extant, celebrated in 472 B.C. the Persian defeat at Salamis eight years earlier. The poet had himself fought in the battle, along with many of his audience; the *choregos* was Pericles. The play is a striking contrast with Shakespeare's fast-moving and wide-ranging 'Histories'. It has neither plot nor characterisation in the ordinary sense. The scene is not the battle itself, but the Persian capital some months later; and at this one point in space and time the whole Persian War is brought in imagination before the audience—the past, through the chorus' account of the expedition and the Messenger's narrative of Salamis; the future, through prophecy by the ghost of Darius. To this point comes the defeated Xerxes, bringing a climax of grief and lamentation. The whole is a masterpiece of pageantry and spectacle conveyed through the spoken word. If we can imagine the production in about 1950 of a play set in Hitler's headquarters at the time of D-day, we may understand something of the effect of the *Persians* in the theatre at Athens.

The rest of the surviving tragedies draw their themes from legend, the story of the remote past, which had a larger place in the Greeks' education and their thoughts than most of their more recent history. Sometimes legend, too, could be given a direct link with the audience, perhaps explaining the origin of some familiar ritual or some other feature of their lives. In the *Eumenides* (458 B.C.) Aeschylus brings Orestes to Athens to be tried for the murder of his mother. Athena, goddess of the city, presides over the court and bids the herald proclaim the opening of the trial:

> Let the Tyrrhenian trumpet, filled with mortal breath,
> Crack the broad heaven, and shake Athens with its voice.[1]

The trumpet sounds, and the whole audience is no longer watching a play, but taking part in the establishment of the court which they still know as the Areopagus.

It is not surprising that appeal to Attic pride or patriotism is a common feature of the playwrights' handling of legend. Athens is portrayed as the champion of the weak and the oppressed, the home of democracy and freedom. In the early years of the Peloponnesian War Euripides uses the old stories as a vehicle for propaganda against Sparta. But more important is the fact that the whole stock of legend from which the dramatists derived their plots was a common heritage, a wealth of material which all felt to be a common possession, although conflicting evidence makes it impossible to judge how far the audience were familiar with the details. The idea of fiction in the theatre was not unknown; it was familiar from comedy, and in the *Poetics* (9) Aristotle mentions a play by Agathon as one of a number of tragedies with invented characters and plot. But evidently the experiment did not last: it was not mere tradition or dislike of change that kept these more or less familiar stories

[1] Translated by Philip Vellacott in Penguin Classics.

of the past as the stuff of tragedy, but a sense that here was the community's richest source for serious drama.

Legend, then, was the storehouse to which the tragic poets normally turned for their plots; but legend already seen in a certain way and moulded into a certain shape. Aeschylus is said to have called his plays 'slices from the great banquets of Homer' (Athenaeus VIII, 347e): by 'Homer' a Greek of his day meant not only the *Iliad* and the *Odyssey*, but all the mass of epic poetry in Homeric style, now lost, which then covered the whole range of mythology and heroic saga. Whether Aeschylus ever used the phrase or not, it states a truth which others echo, and which is basic for the understanding of Greek tragedy. Plato in the *Republic* (595b–c) speaks of Homer as 'the original teacher and guide of the fine company of tragic poets'. Aristotle links tragedy and epic closely together and finds the same elements in both. If we think of Homeric epic not as lines on the printed page but as the Greeks knew it— narrative and speeches recited, almost acted, whether by the boy at school or the rhapsode at the festival—the kinship between this and drama becomes more obvious. What the playwrights found in epic, or in lyric poetry closely related to epic, was not like the raw material which Shakespeare took from Plutarch and elsewhere: it was material already worked, already stamped with features which reappear in the theatre. Although Greek tragedy is far removed from 'epic theatre' in the sense used by Brecht, its main characteristics repeatedly take us back to Homer: its conception of human beings, heroic or humble; the intervention of the gods in human life; man's dignity and his helplessness. All these are strongly present in the *Iliad*, perhaps the greatest of tragedies; and for other elements of fifth-century drama—romantic adventure, ingenuity of plot—we need look no further than the *Odyssey*; while in both poems the combination of swift narrative with the clash of speech and counter-speech prepares us for the texture of the plays. There can be no better background reading for Greek tragedy than the two Homeric epics.

Homer has often been called the Greek Bible. There is some truth in the phrase if the influence of early epic on later life and literature is what we have in mind, but the comparison is misleading if it implies that Homer's works were treated as holy writ. Against emphasis on the epic version of legend as the background to tragedy must be set the equally important point that no version was regarded as 'orthodox'. A feature of Greek religion very relevant to drama is that ritual (including the ritual of the theatre) was fixed and not easily altered, but belief was fluid, variable, ever-changing. The stories of gods and heroes continually took new form, and the chief agents in the process were the poets. The Greek *poietes* means 'maker'; and when Aristotle describes the dramatist as a 'maker of stories' (*Poetics* 9) he is placing him in line with the epic and choral poets who had already made and remade the stories before him.

To us this conception of the playwright's function may seem strange. We do not now rewrite our classics, but leave it to the director to produce new versions by reinterpreting the text. But in the Greek theatre the same themes were repeatedly refashioned: we have the titles of Oedipus plays by twelve different authors, and there may have been more; we know of 56 subjects which were handled by at least two authors, 16 used by 3, 12 by 4, 5 by 5, 3 by 6, and 2 by 7. Amid all the reshaping an essential nucleus was retained: as Aristotle says, Clytemnestra must be killed by Orestes; for Orestes and Aegisthus to go off as friends was possible in comic burlesque of the story, but not in tragedy (*Poetics* 13, 14). How far freedom of invention was carried outside this nucleus we cannot tell. Even for most of the plays that have survived the question is unanswerable, because we know too little of the earlier form of the story in epic or in choral song or in art. But Aristotle's choice of plot as the central feature of drama would be impossible if one play did little more than repeat the plot of another, and some at least of the extant tragedies may go further in giving the legend an original twist than is commonly thought. The *Eumenides* with its trial scene at Athens seems to be Aeschylus' own conclusion to the Orestes story; there is no known model for Sophocles' *Antigone*; and Medea's murder of her children may well be Euripides' own addition. It is clear from the *Frogs* that a large part of the play's interest for the audience was the tension between the familiar and the new. Modern productions might bring us nearer to the original impact of Greek tragedy if the audience were given not a synopsis of the plot, but an account of the story as it was previously known in epic, in choral song, in other plays, and in art.

If we ask *how* the poet shaped his play out of his chosen material, we come near to the heart of dramatic creation as the Greeks saw it. It was not a question of abstract thought, of remodelling the traditional stories to fit a set of abstract ideas. Centuries later Seneca produced Latin dramatisations of the same themes by conscious application of Stoic principles. In Bernard Shaw's works the theory of the Life-Force too often makes itself felt in the play as well as in the preface; and even O'Neill's powerful version of the Orestes legend, *Mourning Becomes Electra*, owes too obvious a debt to Freud. But the fifth-century tragic poets were dramatic artists, not philosophers writing plays, although Euripides is sometimes in danger of falling under this description; and the artist thinks not in abstract terms but in terms of the material he uses, whether it is paint or stone or story. No doubt a variety of influences were at work in the dramatist's mind: local patriotism, religious or moral assumptions or attitudes, whether those of his time or his own; above all, the possibilities and limitations of presentation in the theatre. In studying and analysing his writings today one can separate these factors, and produce essays on the religion of

79

Aeschylus or Euripides' attitude to the Peloponnesian War. But surely the process of dramatisation was just this, that under all these influences the playwright re-saw the story: a new conception of it took shape in his imagination, and this he moulded and adapted until it became a play.

This was the essence of the tragic poet's activity. Rightly, it is the main subject with which Aristotle concerns himself in the *Poetics*. 'When I am writing a play,' said Bernard Shaw in the Postscript to *Back to Methuselah*, 'I never invent a plot: I let the play write itself and shape itself, which it always does even when up to the last moment I do not foresee the way out.' One can well believe that many modern plays are written on the same principle, but it is the opposite of the Greek approach. For the Greek dramatist deliberate shaping of the plot was the all-important task. The primary element in tragedy, its life and soul, says Aristotle, is 'the ordering of the incidents', which must be so arranged that 'if any part is moved or taken away, the whole is dislocated and upset' (*Poetics* 6, 8).

Let us look more closely at this key process of re-fashioning or dramatisation, always remembering that even the extant plays are too various for any generalisation to fit them all; remembering, too, that the dramatic poets wrote *for the theatre*. The texts of plays were available for reading in Athens late in the fifth century: in the *Frogs* (52–3) it was reading Euripides' *Andromeda* that gave Dionysus a longing to fetch the poet back from Hades. But the playwright must have had performance at the festival, participation in the tragic contest, foremost in his mind; and there was no director to whom he could leave problems of presentation while he concentrated on higher things.

The result of dramatising material from epic might well have been a sort of chronicle play, no less loosely knit and filled with incident than epic itself. But none of the surviving tragedies comes under this description, and Aristotle tells us (*Poetics* 18) that anything of this kind was doomed to failure:

All the poets who have dramatised the destruction of Troy in its entirety, and not, like Euripides, only part of it, or the whole of the story of Niobe, and not as Aeschylus did it, have either failed utterly or done badly in the dramatic competitions.[1]

Multiplicity of scenes and sub-plots may be natural in Elizabethan drama, but what suited the Attic theatre described in the previous chapters was just the opposite —concentration on a single event or situation. Here again there was some precedent in Homeric epic itself: the *Iliad* does not cover the whole Trojan War, but has as its central core one episode in the final year of the struggle, the 'wrath of Achilles'. In the theatre the single chosen incident was presented not with additions and digressions in the Homeric style, but in its bare essentials. If the playwright drew his whole trilogy from the same legend, he selected three points in it where conflict rose to a dramatic climax, and created a play, short by our standards, centred on each: the murder of Agamemnon, Orestes' revenge, the trial of Orestes. Otherwise his play was built round a single event within the story: the burial of Polyneices, Oedipus' discovery of the truth. The antecedents of the central incident and its sequel could be referred to or narrated, but the keynote of the action itself, as we saw in the last chapter, was simplicity and unity. The fifth-century dramatists did not have the advantage of having read the *Poetics*, and their plays do not always conform to the philosopher's rules; nevertheless, Greek tragedy at its best (*Agamemnon, King Oedipus, Bacchae*) is what Aristotle implies it should be —not a rambling chronicle, nor just a section of legend brought onto the stage, but a presentation of one incident or close-knit group of incidents transformed into a complete, compact and unified work of art.

By the time of the *Persians* a conventional pattern had become established for the result of this transformation process—a pattern which remained basically the

[1] Translated by T. S. Dorsch in *Classical Literary Criticism* (Penguin Classics).

same, although admitting many variations, throughout the period of the extant plays. Its early history is as obscure as other aspects of the origin of tragedy. Significantly, it reminds us of a ritual liturgy. For the fifth-century audience it was a pattern of sound and movement and spectacle. For us, unable to hear the music or see the dance and the grouping, what remains in the text is a pattern of language, style and metre. Even so, this conventional form common to all the tragedies is perhaps their most remarkable feature for the reader of today.

The basic and obvious framework is alternation between spoken dialogue and choral song: the playwright's task in its simplest form was to divide his brief plot into passages of action, or report of action, separated from each other by choral odes. Hence the sequence which we find in all the plays. The chorus rarely entered at the beginning. The usual opening was a *prologos* ('fore-speech', our 'prologue') spoken before the chorus appeared. It could take various forms: dialogue, a speech by one character (the normal practice of Euripides), or a combination of the two. In any case its purpose was explanation of the situation, all the more necessary when the action was to start near the climax of the story; and even in a dialogue *prologos* improbabilities seem to have been acceptable in the cause of making the explanation clear. Thereafter came the march of the chorus into the *orchestra* and their first song (Greek: *parodos*, already mentioned in Chapter 5 as the name of the passageway by which they entered). The dialogue scene which followed was called an episode (Greek: *epeisodion*, from the coming of an actor to join the chorus); the subsequent choral odes, *stasima*, probably not 'stationary' songs, which would be far from true at any rate of fifth-century practice, but songs sung after the chorus had reached their station. After the last of these the final scene, which Euripides commonly concluded with a 'god out of the machine', was known as the *exodos* ('exit') although originally this may have meant only the few lines sung by the departing chorus to end the performance. Such are the technical terms of tragedy as Aristotle gives them (*Poetics* 12). How widely they were used we do not know, but they confirm the structural convention which we find in the extant dramas. Lengthen the episodes, take away the chorus and replace its songs by a curtain and possibly an interval, and we have a modern play.

This was the basic outline. But formal shape, balance, symmetry played a far larger part in tragedy than this, sometimes in ways which disappear in translation. Reference has already been made to the complex metrical patterning of the choral ode with its corresponding pairs of stanzas. The intricacies of choral rhythm can be understood only by study of the Greek text, and even then, as we have seen, incompletely, in our ignorance of the accompanying music and the dance. More apparent in an English version is the repeated occurrence of symmetrical design within the dialogue scenes. In Sophocles' *Antigone*, for example, a choral song is followed (626) by the entry of Creon's son, Haemon. Creon speaks to the young man in four lines, and receives a four-line reply. Creon then states his case in 42 lines, and after a two-line comment by the chorus-leader, Haemon gives his answer in 41 (or according to some editors, in 42), again with two from the chorus-leader at the end. Father and son each speak two lines, and then follow 28 in which they argue in thrust and counter-thrust, one line each, until four from Creon and the same number from Haemon conclude the quarrel and the son hurries off. Reduced to arithmetic, the scene may sound absurd; watched in the theatre, it is a powerful clash which gains rather than loses from its formal shape.

For the balance of speech against speech, strange though it may seem to us, it is not difficult to find parallels in Greek literature and life. Here again tragedy had ample precedent in Homer, and among fifth-century authors we need look no further than the formal debates which Thucydides uses to explain the motivation of historical events. Law court practice was to allow opponents equal speaking-time by the water-clock. *Stichomythia* ('line-by-line talk') is more difficult to explain, and we can only conjecture that it had a ritual origin. But it is the normal form of conversation in tragedy, often, as in the Haemon scene, following longer speeches. Sometimes in moments of excitement or passion the exchange becomes more rapid and half-lines are used. To maintain the pattern a sentence could be interrupted and its syntax obliged to wait for completion—a point neatly parodied by A. E. Housman in dialogue between the chorus-leader and a newcomer in his *Fragment of a Greek Tragedy*:

Chorus.	Might I then hear at what your presence shoots?
Alcmaeon.	A shepherd's questioned mouth informed me that—
Chorus.	What? For I know not yet what you will say—
Alcmaeon.	Nor will you ever, if you interrupt.
Chorus.	Proceed, and I will hold my speechless tongue.
Alcmaeon.	—This house was Eriphyla's, no one's else.

It is in quick-fire dialogue of this sort that the Greek playwright exploits most effectively one of the chief features of his art—dramatic irony, which is one of the ways in which the audience is given a feeling of participation in the play. Because the audience is aware of the realities of the situation, line after line can have a significance for them which it lacks for one or more of the characters. They are in the secret, and wait with heightened expectancy for the characters to discover the truth. In Euripides' *Iphigenia among the Taurians* Orestes, newly landed on the Black Sea coast, meets his sister, who as priestess must sacrifice all foreigners to Artemis. The audience knows the identity of the pair, knows that the sacrifice would be one more killing within the ill-fated family of Agamemnon; but neither yet recognises the other, although a brilliantly contrived recognition is to come.

Iphigenia.	Your heart is made of gold. You must have come
	From some great seed, to be so true a friend.
	If only the last member of my line

Be such as you! I have a brother living,
Though face to face with him, I should not
know him. . . .

Orestes. Whose hand is it that brings the touch of death?
Iphigenia. My hand—condemned to it by Artemis.
Orestes. Your hand is still too young a hand for that.
Iphigenia. It is the law.
Orestes.   That a woman shall stab men?
Iphigenia. Not that! Oh not the knife! Only the water,
The marking on the forehead—only the water!
Orestes. Whose hand then does the deed, uses the knife?
Iphigenia. Inside the temple—there are men for it.
Orestes. When I am burnt, what happens to my body?
Iphigenia. They seal the ashes in a rocky gorge.
Orestes. I wish my sister's hand might tend my body.
Iphigenia. Since she is far away and cannot hear you
Or be with you to give these services,
I shall attend to them. I am from Argos.
I will do everything that she might do.
                                    (609–31)[1]

These are patterns of balance and symmetry within
the dialogue scenes, matched by the still greater formality
of the choral odes. But as we have seen in the last
chapter, the complexity and variability of the whole
design is increased by passages which cut across the
divisions of chorus and dialogue or song and speech.
Ritual mourning was a normal accompaniment of death
or disaster in Greek life, and inevitably has a large place
in representation of them in the theatre. Hence the
kommos (from a verb meaning 'to beat the breast'), in
which chorus and actor or actors answer each other in
matching stanzas of chanted lamentation—sometimes at
a length that becomes wearisome for the modern reader
or the modern audience. More rarely the same form of
combined song was used to express other emotions, fear
or even joy. Solo singing ('monody') or duets or trios by
the actors were a favourite practice of Euripides, much

[1] Euripides, *Iphigenia in Tauris*, translated by Witter Bynner in
The Complete Greek Tragedies (Chicago University Press).

ridiculed and parodied in comedy. Comparison has already been made between the ancient actor and an operatic star: parts of Euripides' plays must have been nearer to opera than to 'straight' drama as we know it. Most remarkable of all is the Phrygian slave in the *Orestes*, who instead of delivering his news in a normal 'messenger's speech' sings 130 lines of excited lyric punctuated by spoken lines from the leader of the chorus.

Much more could be said about the formal aspect of tragedy. Formal balance is to be found not only in this or that section, but reaching across the play as a whole. An obvious example is Euripides' treatment of the two goddesses in the *Hippolytus*: Aphrodite begins the play, Artemis ends it, and their two pronouncements form a framework enclosing the action. Aphrodite's opening speech is followed by a hymn to Artemis; a choral song on the power of Love precedes Artemis' appearance at the close. Further study of the text brings to light other congruities of metre or style. The overall effect is one for which we can find an analogy more easily in the concert hall than the theatre: a Greek tragedy is like a quartet or symphony, built within the limits of a conventional pattern, yet unique.

Because the general pattern of tragedy had something of the stability of ritual, the impression which the extant plays make on the modern reader is one of a certain sameness, even a certain monotony, of form and style. What is remarkable is the variety of content and theme, the range of dramatic experience, that was achieved within the one general convention. Once again we are confronted with that combination of freedom of imagination with restraint which is characteristic of the Greek theatre, as of all Greek art.

Aristotle goes some distance towards recognising this variety. In his chief attempt to classify plots (*Poetics* 10) he divides them into simple and complex, although to us in comparison with most modern drama all Greek tragedy may seem simple. The essential distinction between his two categories is that in the 'simple' play the action moves continuously in one direction, as in Aeschylus' *Prometheus* and Euripides' *Medea*; whereas 'complex' plots involve changes from ignorance to knowledge or from prosperity to disaster. Best of all, says Aristotle, is the play that includes both recognition (Greek: *anagnorisis*) and reversal (Greek: *peripeteia*), and he cites *King Oedipus* as a masterpiece in which the two are effectively combined. It is true that many of the plays involve a drastic change of fortune, and often this is linked with an unexpected discovery about the identity of one of the characters or about past events: dramatic irony, as we have seen, depends on the temporary existence of illusions which the audience does not share. Scholars have done their utmost to bring all the tragedies within Aristotle's description, but even among those extant there are some which it does not fit. Conjectural reconstruction of others suggests still greater diversity: in spite of the general similarity in subject-matter and in form, it is clear that the dramatists' treatment of the material within that form was far more varied than Aristotle's ruling allows.

It is not the purpose of this book to dwell at length on the differences between the three great tragic poets, but at this point generalisation about them ceases to be valid and some separate treatment becomes necessary. Each has his own use of language, his own way of handling the accepted structure of tragedy; above all, his own approach to the 'making of the story', the 'ordering of the incidents', the refashioning of legend for the theatre.

Although the seven extant works of Aeschylus all come from the last part of his life, they still bear the stamp of his nearness to the choral origins of tragedy. As translators know to their cost, his choral songs have a splendour and complexity of diction scarcely paralleled even by his contemporary, Pindar. They abound in metaphor, in accumulation of epithets, in striking compound words; and the language of the dialogue scenes is almost equally rich and strange. His plays have the stiff grandeur of ritual, and he seems to have been more adventurous than his successors in exploiting the resources of the theatre to make them spectacular. Aeschylus was the foremost dramatiser of legend, in the sense that he took themes direct from epic and choral poetry and adapted them for drama: later playwrights often only remoulded material which he had already brought into the theatre. His normal practice was to present a whole trilogy from the same story; whatever the reason for it, working on this scale clearly suited his tremendous range of vision, which is repeatedly shown in the plays as his poetry carries us in imagination far into the past or into the furthest regions of the known world. Each of his three subjects is handled with a powerful simplicity. He selects for treatment a single climax point in the story, at which a single straightforward conflict is at issue. From the first the climax is always in view: the earlier scenes of the play lead steadily on towards this expected end. The emotion roused in the audience is suspense, all the stronger when they are aware of what is to come.

Let us look at two examples, very different yet both typical: *Seven against Thebes* and *Agamemnon*.

The *Seven against Thebes* was the last part of a Theban trilogy—the first dramatisation, as far as we know, of that story of the family of Laius and Oedipus and Antigone which was constantly rehandled by Greek poets and still provides material for a Cocteau or an Anouilh. Aeschylus saw the legend as one of a royal house stricken by a curse, and for his first two plays, now lost, chose two points at which the blow falls: we know little more of them than we can guess from the titles, *Laius* and *Oedipus*. For the third he selected the fulfilment of the fate called down by Oedipus upon his sons, that they should fight over their heritage and kill each other. They have agreed to rule Thebes for alternate years, but Eteocles at the end of his year has refused to make way for Polyneices, who has brought an army to the seven-gated city to overthrow him.

88

Aeschylus sets his scene not on the battlefield but in an open place in the town. The spectacle of the enemy's approach and the conflict itself is not seen, but conveyed to the audience through description: first by a scout who brings news to Eteocles; by the panic-song of the women of the chorus as they hear (and make us hear, without 'noises off') the approach of the enemy; by the scout again, announcing the disposition of the attacking forces; finally, by a messenger who briefly reports the brothers' fatal duel, before their bodies are brought on for the long scene of mourning that ends the play. Each stage in the sequence carries us on towards the anticipated climax. But Aeschylus' masterstroke is his dramatic use of the city's seven gates. When the scout appears a second time, Eteocles has six warriors in full armour beside him. For each gate the scout tells which enemy leader is posted there and describes the device on his shield; Eteocles in a matching speech allots one of the six to face him, and the man goes off; the chorus chant a prayer for his success. As the symmetrical pattern continues the moment steadily approaches when Polyneices must be named as the seventh attacker and Eteocles must go to face him.

> Who has a stronger right than I? Chief against chief
> I'll match him, brother to brother, enemy to enemy.[1]

The scene lasts several hundred lines, and in another play on the same theme (*Phoenician Women*, 751–2) the more realistic Euripides ridiculed its length:

> A waste of time to tell the name of each,
> With the enemy sitting right beneath our walls.

But for all its perhaps naive simplicity, the *Seven against Thebes* is far more dramatic than the *Phoenician Women*.

In the *Agamemnon*, first play of the *Oresteia*, Aeschylus has devised a version of the legend which carries the drama of suspense to its highest level. Again he sees his theme as the story of an afflicted family, in

[1] Translated by Philip Vellacott in Penguin Classics.

which one crime calls forth another. For his first climax point he chooses the murder of Agamemnon on his return home from the Trojan war. The note of foreboding is struck in the Watchman's opening speech, when he sights from the *skene* roof the beacon that signals the fall of Troy. But scene after scene of mounting suspense passes before the foreboding is fulfilled and Agamemnon meets his fate. The *parodos* recalls the earlier horrors that have led up to this moment. Clytemnestra tells how the chain of beacons brought the news. The first arrival from the returning army is not the king, but a herald who announces his approach and describes the weary years of the siege. The play is nearly half over before Agamemnon arrives with his captive princess, Cassandra, and Clytemnestra persuades him against his will to commit the sin of pride by walking over a crimson carpet to the palace door. Still Cassandra is left before the audience—the prophetess whose lot it was always to foretell the truth but never to be believed. In wild song turning to more sober speech and then again to fury, she tells the unbelieving chorus her vision of the doom of the family from first to last, culminating in the murders still to come—the king's death and her own. She goes in, and only now does the long-expected death-cry come from the palace. No messenger comes out to tell the story: by a stroke of genius, Aeschylus has already told it in advance, shown us the full horror of the blow *before* it falls. The *ekkyklema* is wheeled out with Clytemnestra standing triumphant over her victims.

As Sir John Beazley wrote, 'long and conflicting suspense, a knife-flash of action and that unseen, and then strange revulsion and unease, is the very formula, the very soul, of Aeschylean tragedy'.[1]

Many would choose Aeschylus as the greatest of the Greek dramatists; yet in his work tragedy is still in the

[1] Beazley and Ashmole, *Greek Sculpture and Painting*, p. 38.

making. In Sophocles it becomes an independent art and rises to full maturity. The atmosphere of his plays is no longer dominated by the ritual origins of drama. The part given to the chorus dwindles, although Sophocles' choral odes are some of the finest of all Greek poetry. The dialogue, still poetic, becomes simpler and more natural. The action takes on a form which can fairly be called a 'plot' in our sense of the word: at his best, Sophocles fully justifies Aristotle's view of him as an outstanding master of plot—partly, no doubt, because he is building on Aeschylus' experience, refashioning material which Aeschylus has already worked. Unlike his predecessor, he normally writes plays that stand alone, unconnected with the rest of the trilogy. His theme is a single event, but the unity of his treatment of it is sometimes less obvious than in Aeschylus because he divides it into 'episodes' which have more dramatic weight of their own and are not only steps towards an expected climax. The modern concern with character (of which more later) has even caused the criticism of disunity, of falling into two parts, to be brought against *Ajax*, *Antigone*, and *Women of Trachis*, in which a leading figure in the action dies at an early stage; whereas in fact this early disappearance is confirmation that the poet's main concern lies elsewhere. In Sophocles Aristotle's 'reversal' and 'recognition' are brilliantly exemplified; and with them, dramatic irony. Where Aeschylus leads us steadily though slowly towards the crisis, Sophocles makes sudden twists and turns on the way. We still feel suspense and foreboding, but Sophocles also brings his audience a sensation new in the theatre—the shock of surprise.

Aristotle is right in choosing *King Oedipus* as the outstanding example of Sophocles' artistry, quite apart from the fact that it provides a splendid role for the protagonist. When Oedipus curses the killer of Laius who according to the oracle has brought plague to Thebes, the audience knows that the curse will fall on his own head; and the issue is left in no doubt by the prophecies of Teiresias, who tells the unbelieving king all that is to come. But Oedipus' recognition of the truth and the utter reversal of his fortunes is brought about in no direct or simple Aeschylean manner. Sophocles brilliantly splits the process into a sequence of scenes which each involve some unexpected turn. Jocasta's account of Laius' death, intended to disprove the truth of oracles, stirs a memory in Oedipus and sets him on the road of self-discovery which will prove Apollo right:

> *Oedipus.* My wife, what you have said has troubled me.
> My mind goes back . . . and something in me
> moves . . .
> *Jocasta.* Why? What is the matter? How you turn and
> start!
> *Oedipus.* Did you not say that Laius was killed
> At a place where three roads meet?[1]

Again an oracle seems to have come to nothing when a messenger brings news of the death of Oedipus' supposed father, Polybus; but the man makes a revelation about Oedipus' origins which causes Jocasta to realise the truth and drives her in to her death. A series of such episodes carries us through to the catastrophe. The most remarkable feature of the play is one that makes it a distinctive product of the Greek theatre: it seems full of incident and action, but in fact it is built out of narrative and argument. To quote Waldock (*Sophocles the Dramatist*, p. 168): 'Hardly anything happens, beyond people arriving with news. We watch how the pieces of a puzzle fall one by one into place. Yet can one think of a drama so vibrant with the sense of event?'

Antigone is another masterpiece of report and debate on action which occurs 'off stage'. A very different play, but one equally typical of its author, is *Philoctetes*, written in the last years of his long life on a theme which Aeschylus and Euripides (and perhaps others) had already used before him. Here there is no reporting, not

[1] Sophocles, *Oedipus Rex*, translated by E. F. Watling (Penguin Classics).

a single messenger's speech: all the action takes place in front of the audience. But once again a series of scenes brings unexpected shifts and changes in the plot. The *skene* door represents a cave on the island of Lemnos, but there is no necessity to see here a need for realism, scene-painting and the like: the scene is described in unusual detail at the beginning, set in the imagination of the audience for the rest of the play. On this uninhabited coast Philoctetes was abandoned by his fellow-Greeks on the way to Troy with a festering snake-bite in his foot. Now the Greeks have learned that without the bow and death-bringing arrows of Heracles, which he has with him, they cannot capture Troy. Odysseus and Achilles' son, Neoptolemus, have come to fetch him. Here are three well-matched parts for the actors; and out of the continually changing relations between them Sophocles constructs a drama involving both recognition and reversal, skilfully using the irresistible bow which makes whoever holds it master of the situation.

We know something of the Aeschylus and Euripides versions of the story, and comparison with them illustrates the playwrights' freedom in handling the legend. Both treated Lemnos as inhabited and used a Lemnian chorus, whereas Sophocles intensifies Philoctetes' plight by making it a desert island, and has a chorus of Greek sailors. In Aeschylus, Odysseus stole the bow while Philoctetes was overcome by pain. In Euripides he had Diomedes as companion, and the play was a struggle between them and Trojan envoys for possession of the sick man and his bow, ending in victory for the Greeks. Only Sophocles brought Neoptolemus into the picture, and thereby transformed the story into something approaching a drama of character: central to his plot is the inner conflict in the young man's mind, which ends in his complete rejection of his mission and agreement to take Philoctetes to Greece. The decision is reversed and the story brought back on to the traditional lines by the intervention of Heracles himself, demanding that his weapons shall fulfil their destiny—the only occasion when Sophocles uses the 'god out of the machine'.

Commentators through the ages have given Euripides the reputation of a radical, an innovator. So his contemporaries saw him, if Aristophanes is a good guide. But he is no revolutionary as far as the form of tragedy is concerned. He keeps well within the traditional pattern: in some ways he tends to make it more definite, to mark off its several elements more clearly than before. As mentioned already, the *prologos* in his plays is a set explanatory speech about the past, as it may have been in the early days of tragedy; and this is often balanced at the end by an equally formal statement from a god about the future. Nearly every play has at least one long messenger's report, and the symmetrical balance of speech against speech gives us set oratorical debates in which one speaker answers the other point by point— Jason versus Medea, Clytemnestra versus Electra, Helen versus Hecuba. There is a growing separation between the elaborate poetical diction of the choral odes and the simple, often almost prosaic, language of the dialogue. On the other hand another Euripidean development, not easily grasped from reading him in translation, blurs the distinction between chorus and characters: in the handling of music he was certainly an innovator, and gave his actors a new range of vocal expression by the use of recitative and song.

Euripides seems to have gone even further than Aeschylus or Sophocles in varying the content which he put into this more or less stereotyped form. No doubt the impression is partly due to the simple circumstance that we possess more of his plays: his versatility is seen to be still greater if we study the many 'fragments' and the attempted reconstructions of the works that are lost. But it is clear that in his hands tragedy did become more diverse than ever before. His treatment of legend was remarkably variable in approach—and in the quality of the result. He wrote the worst of the extant plays, as well as several of the best.

The propaganda of one century makes dreary reading in another, especially if there is a gap of thousands of years between. Euripides sometimes comes all too near to mere propaganda, including war propaganda in the early years of the conflict with Sparta. Consider, for example, his *Andromache*, probably written between 428 and 424 B.C., though a scholiast says it was not performed at Athens. The story went that after the fall of Troy Hector's wife became the prize of Achilles' son, Neoptolemus, who presently married the daughter of Menelaus, the Spartan king. It is not unfair to Euripides to think that his main reason for treating this theme was that Andromache's sufferings at the hands of the Spartans gave him good material for a verbal onslaught on the enemy who were then occupying Attica. Menelaus is portrayed as a villain of the deepest dye, his daughter as a spiteful fiend. Andromache rounds on Menelaus in vigorous rhetorical style:

> You Spartans, whom all men do most detest,
> Tricksters in counsel, princes of deceit,
> Weavers of webs of evil, in whose minds
> All's roundabout and crooked, nothing sound,
> It is unjust you prosper so in Greece!

And more to the same effect, relevant to the Peloponnesian War context but not to the world of Homeric legend. Still more out of place is an attack on the dress and habits of Spartan girls. No wonder such an educational background produced a wanton like Helen! Achilles' father, Peleus, tells Menelaus:

> However much she tried,
> No Spartan girl could keep her chastity.
> With young men they go gadding out from home.
> Their dress disordered and their thighs laid bare,
> They race and wrestle with the men—a thing
> I could not tolerate. Any wonder then
> That there's no virtue in your womenfolk?

It is typical of Euripides that about ten years later he could write the *Trojan Women*, a devastating picture of the results of war itself. But the main trend in his later plays is towards the drama of intrigue and adventure. He tends to find themes in the less familiar versions of legend, though he still ensures in the *prologos* that the audience knows what is to come. His plots become more complex, though still simple by Shakespearian or modern standards: he increases the number of characters, and sometimes crowds the play with incidents until its unity is easily lost from sight. *Ion, Iphigenia among the Taurians,* and *Orestes* are striking examples of his ability to bring excitement or romance into the theatre. Furthest of all from the accepted idea of 'tragedy' is *Helen* (412 B.C.), a whimsical near-comedy which has rightly been compared with *The Tempest* or *The Magic Flute.* Most of the plot and two of the main characters appear to be the dramatist's own invention.

In *Andromache* Helen is the Spartan seductress who caused the Trojan War and then prevailed on Menelaus to take her home again. In the *Trojan Women* we see him putting her on ship for Argos, where (he says) she will be put to death. But now in *Helen* Euripides borrows from a choral poet an entirely different and fantastic version of the story, which neither he nor his audience can have taken seriously—and which, incidentally, makes nonsense of the Trojan War. Helen did not go to Troy at all. We find her at the beginning of the play outside a royal palace on the coast of Egypt, explaining that Hermes transported her in a cloud to this spot after the judgment of Paris: to spite Aphrodite, Hera made Paris carry off a mere phantom likeness of Helen, and it is over this that the deluded Greeks and Trojans have been battling outside Troy. Now the king of Egypt is pestering her to marry him. Enter a Greek, Teucer, who (after recovering from the shock of seeing one so like 'the accursed woman') brings her up to date: Troy fell seven years ago; Menelaus and Helen were lost in a storm on their way home. Presently, of course, enter Menelaus, shipwrecked and cast up on the Egyptian

96

shore. Euripides has created a splendid mistaken identity situation, and he exploits it to the full. One ingenious turn in the plot follows another until the Greeks succeed in making their escape from the angry king, and Castor and Pollux (Helen's brothers) appear above the palace to tell him that all that has happened is the will of Zeus!

After reading anything so gay as this, with its patches of sheer comedy and its happy ending, it is difficult to credit Aristotle's remark (*Poetics* 13) that Euripides was criticised for making his plays end in disaster, or his description of him as 'the most tragic of the poets'. Yet the verdict is true. It is Euripides who carries furthest the function of tragedy as Aristotle sees it—to arouse pity and fear. For contrast with *Helen* let us turn briefly to the *Bacchae*, which was written at the end of his life and presented at Athens by his son after his death. The central character played by the protagonist is a god— Dionysus himself, the god of tragedy in whose theatre the play was performed, and whom Aristophanes perhaps in the same year (405 B.C.) represented in the *Frogs* as a comic figure making his way to Hades in the guise of Heracles. In the *Bacchae* Dionysus and his Asiatic women votaries (the chorus) have brought his worship to Thebes, and already the Theban women have caught the fever of his cult and are revelling in Bacchic ecstasy on the slopes of Mount Cithaeron. The mountain is the real centre of the action, continually held before the imagination of the audience; but the *skene* represents the palace of king Pentheus, who resists the god, in Thebes, and once again we have a drama which seems full of incident yet consists largely of argument and report, enveloped in an atmosphere of tension and exhilaration by the wild yet formal beauty of the choral songs. (In this play above all we lose by ignorance of the music and the dance.) The old men Cadmus and Teiresias prepare to go to join the women on the mountain; Dionysus, disguised as his own priest, is made captive by Pentheus but later gains complete ascendancy over him, persuading him to go dressed as a woman to spy on the mountain revelry; two men come with news from the mountain, a herdsman with a report of the miracles he has seen, a messenger with the story of the miraculous fate of Pentheus, torn to pieces by the women with their bare hands. At last the terrible outcome of all that has happened on the mountain comes before us: the women enter, led by Pentheus' mother Agave bearing aloft in triumph a lion-cub's head, as she thinks, until reason returns and she sees it is the head of her son. Whatever the 'meaning' of the *Bacchae*, no Greek tragedy has a climax more pitiful or fearful than this.

So far this chapter has been concerned with the dramatist's choice of material and the shape he gave to it, the pattern and the plots of tragedy. Little has been said about characterisation. This is the priority order which we find in the *Poetics*. 'Tragedy is a representation,' writes Aristotle (6), 'not of men, but of action and life.' 'Tragedies are not performed in order to represent character, although character is involved for the sake of the action.' 'There could not be a tragedy without action, but there could be without character.' 'The plot is the first essential of tragedy, its life-blood, so to speak, and character takes the second place.'[1] Accordingly most of the discussion of tragedy in the *Poetics* is centred on plot, and the treatment of character is given no more than a few paragraphs.

Aristotle may be wrong on many things, but surely here he is right. Schoolboys and students have spent many hours toiling over essays or examination answers on 'Characterisation in Sophocles' or 'The Character of Medea'. Scores of books and articles have been written on the handling of character by the three tragic poets. Some build up an elaborate picture dependent on subtleties for which it is difficult to find justification in the text of the plays. Others, with more reason, point out that little elaboration of character or development of char-

[1] Translated by T. S. Dorsch in *Classical Literary Criticism* (Penguin Classics).

acter is to be found in Greek drama. They tend to assume that the Greeks were trying to do the same thing with their *dramatis personae* as a modern playwright, and failed because their plays were too short or the action too limited. Seen from this angle, the characters in the extant tragedies are oversimple, unsubtle, static. As usual, however, the matter is better approached from the Greeks' own viewpoint than our own: they were doing something different from the dramatist of today, not the same thing less well; and their characterisation (if we can apply the word to them at all) must be seen in a different light.

The twentieth-century playwright is like the twentieth-century public: for him, as for them, individual character is a subject of fascinating interest for its own sake. Our literature (the novel, biography), our newspapers, our television programmes are all evidence of this. How many children Lady Macbeth had may have been irrelevant for Shakespeare, but the modern audience would dearly like to know. It is not surprising that the playwright's characters should often be more important for him than his plot, that he should tend to think of the characters first and the plot afterwards, lovingly dwelling on their idiosyncrasies and allowing them almost to shape the plot for themselves. He tries to see them from within, to *get inside* them—and expects his actors to do the same. In the critics' reviews the same attitude is reflected: the director's and the actors' interpretation of the characters is discussed far more than the author's handling of the plot.

The Greeks of the fifth-century B.C. had no such conception of character; and as we have seen in the previous chapter, no provision for representing it was made in the theatre at Athens. Because it did not exist, the conditions in which the ancient actor worked were not designed for it: the use of masks, the timeless costume, the lack of depth in the acting area, the acting of female parts by men, the limitation to three actors. Even if the protagonist had only one role in each play of a trilogy, could he 'get inside' three star parts, male and female,

99

on the same morning? To understand characterisation in Attic drama it is from here, not from our own preconceptions, that we must start—from the tragic actor, whom Aristotle, significantly enough, does not clearly distinguish from the character he represents. He bears a name —Agamemnon, Helen, Ajax—if the character belongs to the higher ranks of Homeric society; if not, a type-label—messenger, herdsman, nurse. He wears a corresponding mask. Name and mask together may restrict the range of what he can be made to do or say: if he is Odysseus, he can hardly fail to have some of that cunning and resource with which every Greek was familiar from the *Odyssey*. But even for such well-known figures tradition was so flexible that the same character could be very different in different plays, though they might come from the same author. Within certain wide limits the poet was master of the legend: he was at liberty to add to the hero's exploits or invent a different version of them, even to give him a different wife or children.

What else besides name or label, mask and possibly costume defined the actor's role? His facial expression could not change; his movements were stylised rather than realistic. Sometimes others described him, but usually only in the most general terms. Any further impression of the character he portrayed came from what he *did* and what he *said*; and both of these were determined not by the author's thought about the inner workings of the soul of the being he had created, but by the movement of the plot and the pattern of the play. Let us look again at Sophocles' treatment of Haemon. Anouilh in his *Antigone* does what we expect of a modern dramatist: tells the story of how Haemon and Antigone became betrothed; gives them a poignant scene together; makes Haemon protest wildly to Creon against her execution, rush out crying that he cannot live without her, and finally kill himself beside her. All that he does is 'in character', and comes from his love for Antigone. Now the love between them was not excluded from the ancient versions of the story. It may well have been a central feature in the *Antigone* of Euripides

100

(though in his *Phoenician Women* (1675) she would rather murder Creon's son than marry him). Sophocles makes Haemon's love clear in the Messenger's description of his suicide (1237–40):

> While he was conscious he embraced the maiden,
> holding her gently. Last, he gasped out blood,
> red blood on her white cheek.
> Corpse on a corpse he lies. He found his marriage.[1]

But earlier in the play love-interest would have been, as Waldock puts it, 'a troubling irrelevance', blurring the sharp clash between the two isolated figures, Creon and Antigone. She and Haemon have no scene together. Haemon's function when he does appear is to increase Creon's isolation by arguing not as Antigone's lover, but as son against father: and this he does, as we have seen, in speech countering speech and line replying to line.

Especially strange to the modern mind is this last point—the effect on the actor's role of its stylistic context, its place in the metrical and musical pattern. Each form of dramatic utterance in a Greek tragedy—long speech, line-by-line dialogue, lament with the chorus, solo song, and the rest—has its own limits and its own potentialities, and the words spoken or sung may be determined more by these than by the personality of the 'character' who utters them. When the love-sick Phaedra comes out from the palace in Euripides' *Hippolytus* she sings wildly of her longing for the mountain and the hunt; the Nurse questions her, and after many lines of *stichomythia* forces her to tell her secret; Phaedra then makes a surprisingly quiet and considered speech explaining her situation to the chorus. What has happened? 'Her mood has altered,' we may say, with our attention on Phaedra's inner self. 'Having admitted her love, she can now talk of it calmly and rationally.' The actress in a modern production will try to convey this psychological shift by change of facial expression. But

[1] Sophocles, *Antigone*, translated by Elizabeth Wyckoff in *The Complete Greek Tragedies* (Chicago University Press).

what are we to say when we find the same transfer from passion to rational argument repeated in play after play —Medea, for example, wailing and cursing within the palace yet making a cool and self-possessed speech when she comes out; Cassandra, in both *Agamemnon* and *Trojan Women*, turning from inspired ecstasy to sober reasoning?

What has happened can be seen as an alteration of mood, but it must also be recognised as a change of form and style, from song to speech, from one rhythm to another—a change familiar and acceptable to the audience as a normal feature of the pattern of tragedy. In song, lyrical expression of emotion was expected; in an unaccompanied speech, a reasoned statement of the case —the more eloquent and persuasive, the better. When Hippolytus hears that Phaedra loves him, he plunges into a rhetorical tirade against women which makes him seem to us an insufferable prig; but its effective development of the theme may well have won a round of applause from the Athenian audience. Earlier, when the Nurse replies to Phaedra's speech and urges her to accept the universal power of Love, she uses philosophical arguments and mythological precedents which carry her right 'out of character'.

It is above all the minor figures, usually nameless, whose brief appearance takes its colour from their place in the plot and structure of the play. The messenger has no independent psychological existence of his own. He is a voice eloquently narrating a story in vocabulary and style in keeping with the poetic level of the rest of the drama. Though there may be a touch of homeliness and perhaps even colloquialism in what they say, the humble characters of tragedy bear the stamp of the epic tradition no less than its kings and queens. They have little in common with the Porter in *Macbeth* or the red-faced Private Jones, Second Battalion, into whom Anouilh transforms Sophocles' Guard.

The fact remains, however, that Greek tragedy gives us some of the most powerful characters in the history of drama: Aeschylus' Clytemnestra, for example, or

Sophocles' Oedipus, or Euripides' Medea or Hecuba. Their importance for the ancient audience too is shown by the titles of the plays and the early institution of a prize for acting. The existence of these memorable figures does not disprove what has been said about characterisation or the lack of it. In the Japanese Noh drama, far more than in the Attic theatre, interest is concentrated on one main actor, the *shite*: as a rule he alone is masked and splendidly costumed; his long dance is the climax of the performance; the subordinate actor's attention is focused on him; the playing and singing of musicians and chorus are intensified as his role rises to its peak. He is memorable indeed, yet there is no characterisation of him in the modern sense. Here, rather than on the modern Western stage, is the type to which those lordly beings belong who stalk through the plays of Aeschylus, the heroes and heroines of epic brought to life before the eyes of the audience. The same starting point is right for Sophocles and Euripides also, but as time passes other trends, nearer to our own conception of dramatic character, creep in. Character-interest in its own right becomes a central feature in some plays: we have seen how Neoptolemus' mental conflict is the key factor in the plot of Sophocles' *Philoctetes.* Euripides often comes nearer still to seeing his characters in a modern light, looking at Jason or Clytemnestra as human beings with human frailties. But even he is very far— much further than is sometimes claimed—from 'psychological drama'. Miss Dale put the matter admirably in her edition of his *Alcestis* (pp. xxii, xxvii), rejecting 'that school of thought which sees in the creation of character the chief and most original contribution of Euripides to the drama, scanning every turn of incident, every line of dialogue, for little touches to fill in some complex portrait'. 'In a well-constructed Euripidean tragedy,' she writes, 'what controls a succession of situations is not a firmly conceived unity of character but the shape of the whole action, and what determines the development and finesse of each situation is not a desire to paint in the details of a self-portrait but the rhetoric of the situation.' What is said here of Euripides applies to all Greek tragedy. It is not characterisation that is the decisive element, but the poet's organisation of the action and of the various forms of speech and song which make up the pattern of the play.

One other major aspect of the plays, it may be thought, has received far too little attention in this account of them: the religious and philosophical ideas or assumptions of the dramatists. What were their views about the gods? Is it true that their characters are mere puppets in the hands of Fate? How was their outlook related to the changing beliefs that we find elsewhere in fifth-century Greek literature? These questions are the main burden of many books on Greek tragedy, and it is not the object of this one to add to the complex and difficult discussion which such problems have aroused. But early in this chapter a certain attitude was stated which has been implied throughout—that the tragic poets were dramatists, not philosophers; or at any rate dramatists first and philosophers afterwards. Perhaps the point should be restated in the light of what has been said about the way they worked.

A certain outlook was of course inherent in the material which they drew from epic—the assumption, for example, that there are immortal beings who actively intervene in human affairs. Some modern writers have argued that for Aeschylus and Sophocles, at any rate, little more need be said: there is no religious conception or philosophical thought in their works that carries us beyond Homer or his near-contemporary, Hesiod. No doubt this is a healthy reaction against the strange assortment of 'advanced ideas' which misguided ingenuity has sometimes extracted from the plays. But the matter is not so simple. Let us rather say again that when the playwright refashioned epic material, the elements he threw into the crucible of change included the shifting beliefs of his time and his own attitude towards them; and the result that emerged contained such of these ingredients as were suitable and necessary for the whole, whether they were implicit in the handling of the plot or expressed by the characters or chorus. The dramatist's treatment of supernatural forces, like his handling of the characters, was part of the particular vision which he shaped into a particular trilogy or a particular play.

This is not the way the philosopher's mind works; and it is not surprising that none of the tragic poets is ever regarded by Plato or Aristotle or later writers (until near our own day) as a philosopher. Nor is it surprising that each of the three can be convicted of inconsistencies of thought, even on the evidence of the extant plays. The wise and just Zeus of the *Oresteia*, who makes men suffer in order that he may learn, is difficult to reconcile with the arbitrary tyrant of *Prometheus Bound*; and the view that the nature of Zeus changed later in the Prometheus trilogy is a dubious way out. In Sophocles it is perhaps most possible to find a common denominator —his belief in a divine order imperfectly understood by man; but *Women of Trachis* and *Electra* and *Oedipus at Colonus* are strangely different exemplifications of its operation. The most variable of all is again Euripides: the divergent attitudes of his characters towards the gods can be understood only in the context of each play, or even of each scene. In some passages the immortals are attacked as the cause of suffering and disaster, in others it is said they cannot be the source of evil, in yet others their existence is denied altogether. In several of the plays statements are made which undermine the whole legend on which the plot is based. Amid this diversity it is useless to ask whether Euripides believed in the gods. He was a playwright first and secondly a critic of tradition, but not a systematic thinker in any sphere.

The same kind of answer must be given to the question of fate and free will in the plays. The commonest of all misconceptions of Greek tragedy is to regard it as a drama of destiny, in which every move is predetermined and no power of choice or responsibility for events lies with the human characters. As the Chorus puts it in

Anouilh's *Antigone*: 'In a tragedy, nothing is in doubt and everyone's destiny is known. . . . He who kills is as innocent as he who gets killed: it's all a matter of what part you are playing.' Cocteau entitles his dramatisation of the Oedipus legend *The Infernal Machine*:

> Spectator, this machine you see here wound up to the full in such a way that the spring will slowly unwind the whole length of a human life, is one of the most perfect constructed by the infernal gods for the mathematical destruction of a mortal.

That this rigid determinism was not the view of the Greek tragic poets or their audience is surely suggested by the flexibility of the stories which they used. 'When your name is Antigone,' says Anouilh's Chorus, 'there is only one part you can play; and she will have to play hers through to the end.' But he is mistaken. Euripides' *Antigone*, for example, gave her a very different part: we do not know the details of his version, but it is clear that she was not put to death, but was married to Haemon.

Scrutiny of the plays shows that the subject is more complicated and more confused. Many of the plots turn on the fulfilment of oracles, which implies (if we think the matter out) that what was to happen was already fixed when the oracle spoke. Characters and chorus often bewail the inevitability of fate. Yet Snell is clearly right in saying (*Discovery of the Mind*, p. 105) that 'in the plays of Aeschylus personal decision is a central theme'; and that in Euripides (p. 111) 'the human being is made to stand apart from the variegated tapestry of divine and earthly forces, and instead becomes himself the point whence actions and achievements take their origin. His own passions and his own knowledge are the only determining factors; all else is deception and semblance . . . His is a logical continuation of what Aeschylus had begun.'

How are these contradictions to be reconciled? They cannot. The fact is that similar inconsistency on this issue pervades most of world literature, and has always been (and still is) the mental condition of the majority of mankind. When the writers of the Gospels describe Christ's prophecy to Peter, 'Before the cock crow, thou shalt deny me thrice,' they do not imply that Peter's denial of Jesus was made by a puppet who could not have chosen otherwise. Homer's heroes must die on their 'appointed day'; but this does not prevent them from being portrayed as individuals with desires and wills and choices of their own which result in action. If it did, the *Iliad* and its characters would be intolerably dull, instead of being intensely and vividly alive. So it is in Greek tragedy, though the playwrights sometimes show signs of having gone further towards conscious thought on the subject than Homer—references, for example, to a sharing of responsibility between the human characters and supernatural forces. The philosophical discussion of determinism of which these are symptoms arose later in Greek thought: nowhere in the background of fifth-century drama is there a systematic theory of predestination or free will. The lack of it did not upset the Athenian audience, any more than it troubles most of us today. What they would have found unpalatable was the dreariness of plays in which the characters were mere automata manipulated and crushed by the Infernal Machine of Fate.

We are left with the plays not as illustrations of philosophic or theological doctrine, nor as examples of the inexorable working of destiny, but as plays, each a unique creation with its own birth in the poet's imagination and its own dramatic impact. How such particular works of art can have a universal relevance and a universal appeal is a problem which extends beyond the theatre into all art, and which theorists from Aristotle onwards have tried in vain to solve. The question arises in Greek tragedy, as in Shakespeare, with special sharpness, for its themes were and are extraordinary, untypical—irrelevant, it might be thought, to normal human experience. Not every day do sons kill their fathers and marry their mothers, or wives murder their children to spite their husbands. Perhaps we watch such things with fascination on the stage because they crystallise in an extreme form elemental emotional trends and situations which we all recognise as in some degree our own—love and hate within the family, the fury of the woman scorned, the horror of self-discovery. As Waldock says of *King Lear*, 'the elements of it are all around us, every suburb can show its issues in miniature'. Freud believed that there is something of Oedipus in every man, and it was for this reason that he looked to Greek tragedy for labels for the tendencies he found in human psychology. Whatever the explanation, the material used by Greek playwrights still retains its hold on the human mind: the dramatisation of legend which began at Athens has gone on through the ages and still continues in the theatre of today.

8

Orestes' Revenge

AMONG the surviving plays there are three in which we can watch the great tragic poets at work on the same part of the same legend: Aeschylus' *Libation-Bearers* (Greek: *Choephoroi*), Sophocles' *Electra*, and Euripides' *Electra*. A comparison between them will illustrate the wide variety of treatment that could be given to a single theme —the playwrights' differing conceptions of the story, arrangement of the plot, choice and handling of characters and chorus. It is as if we possessed not one *Macbeth* but three, each by a master hand.

The time relation between the three is obviously important. The *Libation-Bearers*, of course, comes first, produced along with the rest of the *Oresteia* trilogy in 458 B.C. The two *Electras*, as we shall see, both bear obvious relationships to the Aeschylean version whether by similarity or contrast, yet they are separated from it by a gap of some forty years: both probably belong to the decade 420–410 B.C., though there is no certainty about the exact date of either. A reference to the *Libation-Bearers* in Aristophanes (*Clouds* 534–6) suggests a possible explanation of the gap—a revival of Aeschylus' play a year or two before 420 B.C., which placed it afresh in the mind of the Athenian audience and prompted the two new treatments of the theme. It seems likely that Euripides' came first, and Sophocles' a few years later; and this is the order in which they will be discussed in this chapter. But if the reverse is true, the contrast between the plays is still illuminating. A fourth completes the picture—Euripides' *Orestes*, which in 408 B.C. gave him the last word in the strange dialogue of version and counter-version which these plays present.

The story of Agamemnon's return home and its sequel must have been well known to the audience that gathered for the City Dionysia in 458 B.C. But it was not one story: even the surviving remains of literature and art show that various versions were current. The legend makes its first appearance in several passages of the *Odyssey*, which themselves do not completely agree; by putting them together we gain a more or less consistent Homeric account. While Agamemnon, lord of Mycenae, was away at the Trojan war, his queen, Clytemnestra, was seduced by his cousin, Aegisthus; and when the king returned with the captive Trojan princess, Cassandra, they were killed. His son Orestes, meanwhile, had fled or been taken to Athens. Then, to quote Alexander Pope's translation of *Odyssey* III, 304–10:

> Seven years, the traitor rich Mycenae swayed,
> And his stern rule the groaning land obey'd;
> The eighth, from Athens to his realm restored,
> Orestes brandish'd the avenging sword,
> Slew the dire pair, and gave to funeral flame
> The vile assassin, and adulterous dame.

Pope's version is vivid, but (as often) incorrect. The Greek tells that Orestes killed Aegisthus and made a funeral feast over him and his mother. How she died is not stated. No blame is attached to Orestes. There is no suggestion of guilt in his revenge, no mention of Furies. He is noble Orestes, the heroic son who did his duty. Indeed the main reason why the story is told in the *Odyssey* is that here is a model for Odysseus' young son, Telemachus, to follow; and the most likely explanation of the poem's reticence on Clytemnestra's death is its inappropriateness in this context. Telemachus must seek vengeance against the male usurpers of his father's substance: his mother Penelope is no Clytemnestra, but an outstanding example of the faithful wife.

Electra, it will be noted, does not appear in Homer, although Agamemnon has three daughters with other names in the *Iliad*. She seems to have been first mentioned in poetry of the seventh century: one poet, Xanthus, gave the reason for her name—she was the daughter who knew no marriage-bed (Greek: *lektron*). Another absentee from the Odyssey account is Orestes' companion, Pylades, who came into the story as it was told in a later epic (now lost) on the returns of the heroes from Troy. His entry implies that Orestes' boyhood refuge must have been the neighbourhood of Delphi, not Athens; and this hint of Apollo's oracle in the background prepares us for the other version which, after the *Odyssey*, must have been best known to Aeschylus and his contemporaries—the *Oresteia* of Stesichorus, a long lyric narrative poem probably written early in the sixth century, of which only a few fragments now survive. In these we find new features which we shall meet again in the plays: Orestes' nurse; an ominous dream which came to Clytemnestra before her death; most important of all, the protection of Orestes by the bow of Apollo against the pursuing Furies roused by his mother's murder. The question of guilt has cast its shadow over the story of heroic revenge.

In art the representations of the legend range from crude portrayals in the seventh century to fine pictures of the deaths of Agamemnon and Aegisthus on a winebowl which must be close in date to Aeschylus' trilogy. Orestes' revenge was the popular subject, especially in Attic red-figure vases about 500 B.C. Aegisthus is regularly the victim; Orestes is the killer but Electra is there; Clytemnestra tries to prevent the murder but is held back.[1] It seems likely that few stories of the heroic past were as familiar to the Athenian public as this.

As far as we know, Aeschylus was the first to bring this familiar material into the theatre and shape it into dramatic form. His conception of it was on a typically grand scale, reaching far back into the early history of Agamemnon's family, and looking beyond Orestes'

[1] For recent views on representations in art, see E. Vermeule, *American Journal of Archaeology*, 1966, pp. 1–22; M. I. Davies, *Bulletin de Correspondance Hellénique*, 1969, 214–60.

revenge for an end to the grim sequence of crime answered by crime. We have already seen that the three climax points which he chose for his trilogy were the murder of Agamemnon, the vengeance of Orestes, and his trial at Athens—possibly the playwright's own addition to the story. Something has been said of the *Agamemnon*. The *Libation-Bearers* must be seen in close relation to it: the dead king haunts the second play with an unseen presence almost stronger than his living and visible role in the first; Clytemnestra the murderess becomes Orestes' chief victim, while Aegisthus, so prominent in Homer's account and in art, now plays a secondary part. The theme of guilt centred on the killing of husband and mother binds the whole trilogy together, leading from the first play through the second to the third.

As in the *Agamemnon*, the *skene* in the *Libation-Bearers* represents the royal palace at Argos. A simple wooden structure near the façade stands for Agamemnon's tomb. Homer had set the story in Mycenae; Stesichorus, in Sparta. Aeschylus' choice of Argos has a political motive: it will enable him to refer at the end of the trilogy to the new alliance between Argos and Athens. Here Orestes must come, unknown and unsuspected, gain entry to the palace, and kill his father's murderer—a series of incidents credible enough in narrative, but not easily devised in the theatre. Two thousand years later, when the Elizabethan playwright John Pickeryng introduced the story into English drama, he solved the problem by giving 'Horestes' an army of a thousand men and creating a stage battle in vigorous Elizabethan style. In Aeschylus' version the only allies available for Orestes, apart from a few attendants, are Pylades, Electra, and the Chorus.

Here was a problem of plot which each of the three tragic poets, as we shall see, solved in his own way. It is typical of Aeschylus that he left it till late in the play, when a burst of swift action brings the climax. All the first half of the drama is given to Orestes' meeting with his sister, and this itself is handled in a way remarkable to us. A modern playwright would surely bring Electra on first, and then would come the expected entry of Orestes. But Aeschylus' version begins with Orestes (the protagonist), who enters with Pylades (the third actor) to lay a lock of his hair on his father's tomb. When Electra (the second actor) and the chorus come, Orestes and Pylades stand aside; but they remain visible to the audience throughout. As usual, the audience is in the secret from the first: there is room for dramatic irony, but none for surprise.

The means of recognition, when it eventually takes place, are elementary: the lock of hair, which matches Electra's own; footprints by the tomb, which fit with hers; an embroidered cloak Orestes wears, which she once worked. Only the last of these clues will bear examination from a realistic standpoint. But Aeschylus' main concern in this part of the play is not the mechanics of recognition, but something quite other. From one point of view it is the religious aspect of the story; but its impact on the audience in the theatre is the creation of atmosphere, of a mounting tension which leads up to the swift and dramatic climax.

Aeschylus takes from Stesichorus the idea of Clytemnestra's dream. It suited his dramatic purpose as a foreboding of things to come, and because it could be used as a means of placing the meeting of Orestes and Electra at Agamemnon's tomb, where our attention is concentrated on the link between the present and the past. Electra has been sent by her mother with offerings to appease Agamemnon's spirit. A terracotta relief found on the island of Melos shows her at the tomb with an old woman—the nurse—beside her. But Aeschylus does better: he gives her as companion libation-bearers the whole chorus of slave women, and she and they together swell out this preparatory first half of the drama with a great pattern not only of words but of spectacle, music and dance, setting the act of recognition in a wider ritual context which, significantly, gives the play its name. The scene is the Aeschylean equivalent of Hamlet's meeting with his father's ghost: the contrast between its formal, static structure and Shakespeare's encounters on the battlements illustrates well the difference between Greek and Elizabethan drama.

While Orestes is making the opening speech, the chorus begin their entry with the flute-player; and when he and Pylades have drawn aside, they chant a *parodos* which tells why they have come and strikes a note of foreboding for the guilt-ridden house. Electra has entered with them, and in dialogue with the chorus-leader she changes their errand: their plea to Agamemnon shall be for revenge, and for the return of Orestes. With this prayer the libations are poured, and the chorus sing a brief song calling for a strong avenger to appear. Only now, as if in answer to the prayer, Electra sees the lock of hair and the footprints; Orestes comes forward with Pylades, quickly convinces her that he is indeed her brother, and describes Apollo's command of vengeance. If he does not obey, the god has warned him of the horrors he will suffer from the Furies let loose by his father's anger.

Now we expect speedy action. But it is still delayed, just as Agamemnon's death in the first play of the trilogy is delayed by the long Cassandra scene. Orestes' speech was a preparation not for action, but for a long formal *kommos* in which brother and sister and chorus chant in turn, invoking the spirit of the dead king, ascending a spiral of anticipation and suspense which must culminate in action. At the close of the invocation the chorus-leader tells Orestes of his mother's dream and Orestes interprets it: he himself must be her murderer. At last he explains the means by which he and Pylades will gain entry to the palace: they will pretend to be strangers from Phocis, the region around Delphi. All is now set for the revenge. Electra goes in through the *skene* door, Orestes and Pylades go off to the side, and the chorus sing and dance an ode on other women famous in story, like Clytemnestra, for their misdeeds: such crimes must bring vengeance in the end.

Now that all is ready and suspense has reached breaking-point, events move fast. Orestes re-enters with Pylades and attendants, and knocks at the palace door.

The voice of a servant replies from within, but soon Clytemnestra comes out (the second actor, who till now has been Electra). To her Orestes tells his story: he brings from Phocis the news that Orestes is dead, his ashes already in their funeral urn. The queen invites the strangers into the palace. The action has moved out of sight inside the *skene*, and the poet uses the chorus to maintain tension among the audience over what is happening within. As they sing a prayer for victory, Orestes' old nurse hurries out in tears (as the chorus-leader tells us), sent by the queen to fetch Aegisthus, who is away from home. To use a nurse on such an errand is unusual, but Aeschylus has chosen well. For his purpose he needs a messenger who is loyal to Orestes; and she shows her love for him in a speech that fits her calling, going back to the baby boy she reared before he went away. For once the chorus-leader makes a bold intervention in the plot: she must change her message and tell Aegisthus to come not with a bodyguard, but alone. When she has gone, the song of the chorus is a long supplication to the gods for Orestes' success. Aegisthus comes and goes within, and as the chorus prays for the knife to strike home the usurper's death-cry rings out across the theatre.

So the play reaches its climax, involving action that strains the three-actor system to the utmost. In quick succession a servant appears in the doorway, shouting that Aegisthus is dead and calling for Clytemnestra; then, the queen herself; and as she sends the servant for a weapon, Orestes, who launches into bitter argument with his mother but hesitates to strike her down. He appeals to Pylades, who must also have come out.

Orestes. Pylades, what shall I do? To kill a mother is
      terrible,
      Shall I show mercy?
Pylades.   Where then are Apollo's words,
      His Pythian oracles? What becomes of men's
      sworn oaths?
      Make all men living your enemies, but not the
      gods.

Orestes. I uphold your judgment; your advice is good.
    (*To Clytemnestra*) Come on;
    I mean to kill you close beside him. While he lived
    You preferred him to my father. Sleep with him in
    death.[1]

The third actor, whom the audience has already watched
as Pylades and as the Nurse (unless this part was done by
the second, along with Electra and Clytemnestra) here
reappears as the servant and then, by a lightning change,
as Pylades once more. It seems remarkable that
Aeschylus should create this difficulty by making Pylades
speak at this point the only lines he is given in the play;
without them, the part could have been taken by a mute
actor. In any case this solitary utterance is strange. What
modern dramatist, having decided to include such a
figure, could have refrained from giving him more to do,
or at any rate more to say? But in this and in all his plays
Aeschylus uses his characters for the purpose for which
he needs them, and no more. He does not 'characterise'
Pylades, but simply makes him fulfil his essential function. He is the spokesman of Apollo, the voice of the god.
Because he is silent throughout the rest of the play we
know nothing of his character, but his words come upon
us, as Kitto says, like a thunderclap.

After some twenty lines of *stichomythia*, all the more
tense for their line-by-line pattern, Orestes drives the
queen in to her death, and the chorus sing an ode of joy
and triumph. The great *skene* door opens once more and
the *ekkyklema* is pushed out, with Orestes standing
over the bodies of Aegisthus and Clytemnestra. The
audience cannot fail to see the parallel with the tableau
brought before them an hour or so earlier in the trilogy
—the queen with the bodies of Agamemnon and Cassandra. To make the point doubly clear Orestes holds up
the robe which Clytemnestra also displayed, the net in
which she entangled her victims. But as he speaks of her
guilt and her punishment his tone changes to bewilder-
ment and fear, and he describes with horror the

[1] Translated by Philip Vellacott in Penguin Classics.

116

approaching Furies whom the shedding of her blood has roused. He rushes off to seek refuge at Delphi, and the chorus' exit song asks when the story of crime and death will end. As the opening scenes of the play linked it with the *Agamemnon*, so its close prepares the way for the *Eumenides*.

The contrast between the *Libation-Bearers* and Euripides' *Electra* is a striking illustration of the range of Attic tragedy, for all its limitations of form and subject-matter. Euripides' play is original in all but the barest essentials: the plot, the characters, the whole significance of the story have been seen in a new light. But Euripides has not simply started afresh. References in his *Electra* to details of Aeschylus' version confirm what is evident from the play as a whole—that whether the *Libation-Bearers* had recently been revived or not, he wrote his new dramatisation of the legend as a deliberate rejection of the Aeschylean approach.

His solution of the problem of getting the avengers inside the palace is to abandon it altogether. A question from Orestes on how he is to accomplish his purpose evokes the answer (615): 'Not by going inside the walls, however much you wished it.' The murders must take place elsewhere, and the palace-setting must go. Euripides has made a brilliant stroke in devising a substitute. The *skene* becomes a cottage in the Argive hills where Electra is living: Aegisthus has married her off to a Peasant, but she remains a virgin. The change not only opens up a series of new possibilities for the plot of the play; it also creates a different Electra, introduces in the Peasant a humble figure whose simple honesty contrasts with the warped mentality of the 'heroic' characters, and adds to the horror of the story by setting its sordid violence in surroundings which the audience would recognise as not far different from their own.

The new note is struck in the *prologos*. It is the third actor as the Peasant who opens the play, rapidly recalling

117

the past and explaining in more detail the present. At the end of his speech Electra (the protagonist) comes from the cottage—a slave-like figure with short-haired mask and ragged dress, carrying a jar to fetch water from the spring. When they have gone, enter Orestes (the second actor) and Pylades (who remains mute throughout the play). They had already visited Agamemnon's grave and left a lock of hair there and sacrificed a lamb. As Orestes speaks, Electra returns with her jar of water and they draw aside. A piece of Euripidean patterning follows, typical of his combination of characters and chorus: Electra sings (and dances?) a long solo, telling who she is and describing her plight; the chorus of country women enter and in a variation on the same rhythm sing in alternation with her. There is to be a festival at Argos, they say, and they will lend her a dress to wear. But Electra will not go. She mourns for her absent brother and her own lot.

> And I! I in a peasant's hut
> waste my life like wax in the sun,
> thrust and barred from my father's home
> to a scarred mountain exile
> while my mother rolls in her bloody bed
> and plays at love with a stranger.[1]

With both Orestes and Electra before them, the audience now awaits the recognition scene: like what they have watched already, it will surely be different from Aeschylus. They are not disappointed, but the recognition itself is slow to come. First there is long *stichomythia* between brother and sister, full of dramatic irony. The Peasant enters, giving Orestes an opportunity for a sententious speech (hardly 'in character') on the falsity of wealth as a test of men. He invites the strangers into the cottage, and Electra sends him to fetch a shepherd who can bring something to be cooked for them—

[1] This quotation and those on p. 119 are from the translation by Emily Townsend Vermeule in *Complete Greek Tragedies* (Chicago University Press).

the Old Man who saved Orestes as a boy, Euripides' version of Agamemnon's faithful herald Talthybius. The Chorus sing a romantic ode on Achilles linked with the play only in the last few lines, and then the Old Man (the third actor, previously the Peasant) comes with a lamb and cheese and wine. On his way he has passed Agamemnon's grave and seen the lock of hair and the footprints. Can they belong to Orestes? Electra rejects both clues with ridicule, along with the Old Man's suggestion that Orestes might still be wearing the cloth she once wove:

If a little girl's hand
could weave, how could a growing boy still wear that cloth
unless his shirt and tunic lengthened with his legs?

After these sallies against Aeschylus in the cause of realism Euripides must produce a realistic means of recognition himself, as soon as Orestes appears: he does it by making the Old Man recognise him by a boyhood scar.

In devising the revenge Euripides agrees with Aeschylus on one all-important point: it is the murder of Clytemnestra that matters most and must be the climax; Aegisthus is to be the first victim. The Old Man reports that he happens to be near by with a few slaves preparing a sacrifice: he will guide Orestes to the place. In a few lines they pray to the gods and to Agamemnon for victory, but there is to be none of the lengthy ritual of the *Libation-Bearers*.

Electra. Did you hear us, terrible victim of our mother's love?
Old Man. All, your father hears all, I know. Time now to march.

After the men have gone and the chorus has sung another romantic song which has little relevance, a messenger (the third actor again) enters and tells at length the dramatic story of how Aegisthus died, struck down from behind as he bent over the sacrifice. As the chorus and Electra dance for joy, Orestes and Pylades return with the corpse. Speeches of praise over the dead were a familiar feature of life in war-torn Athens. Electra addresses to the dead Aegisthus a long speech of denunciation and hate.

The body is carried into the cottage, and Clytemnestra is seen approaching. Electra has lured her into the trap by a false message that a grandchild has been born. When Orestes' nerve fails at the sight of her, no reminder of the oracle comes from Pylades: Orestes now sees Apollo's command as brutal and blind. It is Electra who steels his wavering resolve and sends him and Pylades into the cottage to await their chance. The queen (the third actor yet once more) arrives in a carriage with Trojan slave girls, and a set debate between the two women follows in which each makes a speech of forty lines. Electra talks of her child and persuades her mother to go within and make due sacrifice for the birth. As the chorus recall in excited song how she killed Agamemnon, her death shrieks are heard. But no messenger comes out through the *skene* door; instead, the *ekkyklema*, with Electra, Orestes and Pylades standing over the bodies of their victims. In place of the expected messenger's speech, brother and sister and chorus join in a song of lamentation at the horror of what has been done, telling each detail of Clytemnestra's death. Electra, so hard before, is no less broken and guilt-stricken than Orestes.

The tense operatic scene is typical of Euripides, and so is his way of breaking the tension and ending the play. With the help of the theatre crane Castor and Pollux, twin sea-gods and divine brothers of Clytemnestra, appear above the *skene*. Castor (the third actor in his fifth part) proclaims that what has happened must be accepted and goes on to foretell the future, bringing us back with a jolt into the story as told by Aeschylus. Orestes must leave Argos, and will be pursued by the Furies until he is tried and acquitted at Athens. Aegisthus will be buried by the people of Argos, Clytemnestra by her sister Helen, just back with Menelaus from Egypt—for she never went to Troy. Pylades must marry Electra, and they must take the Peasant to Phocis and there make him rich. Under questioning, Castor assigns the blame for the past to fate and Apollo's 'unwise utterance'. He warns that the Furies are approaching, and Orestes and Electra go their separate ways.

This extraordinary play must have shocked Euripides' contemporaries. It is not only a contrast with Aeschylus: it rejects the whole epic conception of legend. Euripides has redrawn the characters to suit his radically new version of the story, and in so doing has reduced them from their heroic stature. Clytemnestra is no super-woman but a shallow, snobbish creature, full of excuses for the past and fearful for the future—a sorry victim for so brutal a revenge. Orestes, pictured by Electra as a romantic hero, proves to be nervous, planless, incapable of action unless the Old Man devises it and his sister prevents him from drawing back. Electra, the dominant character, is embittered and hard, completely callous in planning her mother's murder; but she too breaks when the blow is struck. All compare badly with the Peasant, the one attractive figure in the play.

This is one aspect of the poet's originality, closely bound up with the novelty of his plot. But the play raises a more radical question. What has happened to the legend? In a sense, Euripides has treated it with a new realistic approach, rejecting improbabilities and making its incidents credible, bringing its characters down to earth. Some of the dialogue scenes come as near to realism as the conventions of the Attic theatre and the general pattern of tragedy would allow, so that at times Euripides' version of the story is the most powerful of the three. Yet the impact of this realism of speech and action is cancelled, as it were, by being set in a frame-work which reduces all legend to fantasy. The two long choral odes use legendary narrative as romantic orna-ment, tied by the slenderest of threads to the plot. In the second, the chorus openly express disbelief in the myth they have told; but frightening fables are useful, and

Clytemnestra might have done well to remember them! The 'gods out of the machine' at the end take us back into the realm of make-believe: we are left feeling that the horrors we have heard and watched were just a tale after all, no more credible than the story of a phantom Helen sent to Troy.

We cannot be certain that Sophocles was the last to produce his version of the story, and it can well be appreciated without being related to the other two. It is more self-contained than either of them, and makes its own powerful impact. Nevertheless, its effectiveness is increased if it is seen in its probable historical context— as a reply to Euripides, a rejection of his innovations, a reassertion of what he had set aside. Like Euripides, Sophocles presented not a trilogy on the theme, but a single play, with the same title. It was a direct challenge. Euripides had moved far from the epic point of view. Sophocles returns to it, going back not so much to Stesichorus but to the *Odyssey*: in his version action and characters are on the heroic plane. Euripides had produced a repudiation of Aeschylus. Sophocles does not bring back the whole Aeschylean conception of the legend, but reinstates and uses afresh the main elements of his plot—Orestes' plan for entry to the Palace, the lock of hair, Clytemnestra's dream, and the rest. The result is a play which has led to endless scholarly argument about its author's real attitude to the matricide, but which theatrically is the most skilful of the three and in *Electra* provides the protagonist with one of the greatest roles in all Greek tragedy.

The beginning of the play casts aside Euripides and takes the audience back to Aeschylus. The *skene* once more represents a palace, as we learn in the first few lines: this time, not at Argos but at Mycenae, Homer's setting for the story. As in the *Libation-Bearers*, the first to enter are Orestes (the second actor) and the silent Pylades, but with them comes Orestes' old Tutor (the third actor), in whom we recognise Talthybius again. His opening speech tells us he is Orestes' link with the past —the loyal servant to whom Electra once entrusted her brother, and who from that day has cherished and reared him for this moment of revenge. Now is the time for action, he says; and Orestes quickly runs over their plan. He has learnt from Apollo's oracle not the need for revenge, which he has known since childhood, but the way to success: it must be done by stealth. The Old Man must enter the house and tell the story of Orestes' death. Orestes and Pylades will go meanwhile to Agamemnon's tomb, pour libations there and leave a lock of hair, and return with a funeral urn—Orestes' ashes—to confirm the Tutor's story. Electra's voice cries out from inside the house, and as she enters from the *skene* the men depart.

Sophocles has chosen (for good reason, as we shall see) to put the disclosure of the plan of action in this opening scene, not halfway through the play like Aeschylus. But much has to happen before the Tutor comes to the palace with his tale: not the recognition; nor any building up of tension and atmosphere by ritual at Agamemnon's grave, now 'off-stage'; but portrayal of the situation into which Orestes has come and the characters involved in it—above all, of Electra herself. As in Euripides, she comes in singing a lament, which soon gives way to a long *kommos* between her and the chorus of women of Mycenae, and then to a reasoned speech describing her plight. The scene strikes the keynote of the play. Here is another Antigone, driven to a single-minded hatred and resolve by the complete vileness of Aegisthus and her mother

—if mother I should call her,
this woman that sleeps with him.[1]

No counsels of moderation from the chorus can touch her fanatical determination: she will not falter when the

[1] All quotations from Sophocles' *Electra* are from David Grene's translation in *The Complete Greek Tragedies* (Chicago University Press).

moment comes. The resemblance to Antigone is strengthened when Electra's sister Chrysothemis (the third
actor) enters—the advocate of good sense against high
principle, like Ismene in the earlier play. After an
ominous dream Clytemnestra has sent her with offerings
for Agamemnon's grave, and on her way she has come to
warn Electra of a new ordeal planned for her: when
Aegisthus comes back (it has already been revealed that
he is away from home) she will be imprisoned in an
underground cave. 'The sooner the better' is Electra's
response; and she persuades Chrysothemis to offer at the
tomb not her mother's libations but locks of their hair,
with a prayer for Orestes' return.

After a short choral song, the queen herself enters
from the palace (the second actor, whose other role in the
play is Orestes). The slave-girl with her carries offerings
for Apollo, whose altar or statue stands near the *skene*
door. In speech answered by speech she claims that
Agamemnon's death was justified by the sacrifice of
Iphigenia, and Electra denies it. The bitter clash ends
with Clytemnestra's prayer to the god that she may live
out her life in continued prosperity

> and with such children
> as do not hate me nor cause bitter pain.

The immediate answer to her prayer is the entry of the
Tutor, initiating the action by her other children which
will bring her death.

The Tutor makes his announcement: Orestes is dead.
Before the queen can speak, a cry comes from Electra:

> O God, O God! This is the day I die.

Now it is clear why Sophocles diverged from Aeschylus
and put the plan for the false message at the beginning
of the play. Although the audience is included in the
secret, Electra is not: she believes her brother is dead and
her hopes finished. After Aeschylus' unconvincing recognition scene and Euripides' mockery of it, Sophocles has

devised a means of doing far better than either. He has created a situation in which (to revert to Aristotle) reversal and recognition combine, and dramatic irony is at its most effective.

The Tutor's brief statement of his news is followed by a long narrative of the chariot race at Delphi in which Orestes was killed—a 'messenger's speech' so powerful that the audience almost forgets its falsity for the moment and feels to the full its impact on Electra. Clytemnestra goes into the palace, exultant, and the Tutor with her; and Electra and chorus-leader join in a song of grief. Suddenly Chrysothemis hurries joyfully in. She has been to Agamemnon's grave, seen there new-spilt milk and a wreath and a lock of hair: surely Orestes must have come back at last. Electra tells her the 'truth' and now, more Antigone-like than ever, declares they must achieve their revenge alone. If Chrysothemis will not help her, *she* will do it. Her sister goes, and she stands a solitary figure in front of the *skene* while the chorus sing an ode in which they call on the dead king to heed her loneliness.

> Electra, betrayed, alone,
> is down in the waves of sorrow,
> constantly bewailing her father's fate,
> like the nightingale lamenting.
> She takes no thought of death;
> she is ready to leave the light
> if only she can kill
> the two Furies of her house.
> Was there ever one so noble
> born of a noble house?

At this climax of emphasis on her isolation Orestes enters with Pylades and their attendants. As arranged with the Tutor in the opening scene, they bring with them the urn that contains Orestes' ashes. It was mentioned in Aeschylus: now it has become a potent stage property. Electra, still unknown to the newcomers, takes it from them and mourns over the dead Orestes while the living Orestes stands beside her. Only when the chorus-leader addresses her by name does her brother realise who she is and in *stichomythia* gradually reveal himself, convincing her with Agamemnon's signet ring.

Their rejoicing is interrupted by the Tutor's entry from the palace. No time for long speeches now: the men must go in and act, while Clytemnestra is alone. Again Electra is left with the chorus, this time in eager anticipation. Now it is she who prays to Apollo: she imagines what is going on inside the palace, and as Clytemnestra's cries and appeals for pity come from within, her daughter relentlessly urges Orestes on: 'Strike, if you have strength, again!' No messenger speech follows, no display of the body, no lamentation. Nothing is done that could arouse sympathy for Clytemnestra. When Orestes emerges with Pylades he says all is well, 'if well Apollo prophesied'; and Electra scarcely has time to ask him 'Is the wretch dead?' before Aegisthus approaches and the two men go back into the house. The scene is set for the dramatic climax of the play.

Aegisthus has heard the news of Orestes' death. He questions Electra.

Aegisthus. Where are the strangers then? Tell me that.
Electra. Inside. They have found their hostess very kind.
Aegisthus. And do they genuinely report his death?
Electra. Better than that. They have brought himself, not news.
Aegisthus. Can I then see the body in plain sight?
Electra. You can indeed. It is an ugly sight.

Aegisthus calls for the door to be opened and the corpse displayed, so that all may know who is master now. So once again, as in Aeschylus and Euripides, the *ekkyklema* is used, but to very different purpose. On it stand the 'strangers' beside a covered corpse. Aegisthus commands that the cover be removed.

Orestes. Touch it yourself. This body is not mine,
it is only yours—to see and greet with love.

Aegisthus. True. I accept that. (*To Electra*) Will you call
out Clytemnestra if she is at home?
Orestes.   She is near you.
You need not look elsewhere.
Aegisthus (*lifting the cover*). What do I see?
Orestes.   Something you fear? Do you not know the face?

In a moment Aegisthus realises the trap into which he
has fallen. When he pleads for time, it is Electra who
urges swift action. Orestes drives the usurper in to his
death, and the chorus chant as they leave the orchestra:

> O race of Atreus, how many sufferings
> were yours before you came at last so hardly
> to freedom, perfected by this day's deed.

The long story of crime and horror is apparently complete. There is no reference to things to come, no talk
of Furies or of Orestes facing trial. It was Euripides who
some years later produced a sequel in his *Orestes*, invent-
ing a lurid melodrama of a 'hero' driven mad by Furies
(or hallucinations?), condemned to death with his ruth-
less sister by the people of Argos, and prevented from
further crime only by the incredible intervention of
Apollo 'out of the machine'. Euripides' two plays have
this in common with the *Libation-Bearers*, that they give
us some grasp of their author's attitude towards his
theme. Sophocles' version leaves us far more uncertain
of his conception of the legend; just how uncertain, a
few illustrations from modern comment will show. Jebb:
'It is the bright influence of Apollo that prevails from
the first.' Sheppard: Orestes' tragedy is his misuse and
misunderstanding of the oracle. Lesky: 'The drama of a
human soul whose courage leads her from anguish and
despair to liberation. . . . The way is open to a secure
future.' Thomson: 'Electra's hope has been fulfilled, she
has won her deliverance, but the result is her utter deso-
lation.' Murray: 'A combination of matricide and good
spirits.' Kitto: 'Sombre and unrelieved beyond any other
play of Sophocles.' Waldock: 'To the unprejudiced eye

there is simply no problem at all.' In describing Sophocles' play a certain approach to it has been adopted, but it is not the purpose of this chapter to add to the welter of controversy on its 'meaning'. One thing must surely be universally agreed: that it is a dramatic masterpiece, an outstanding example of what the Greek theatre could achieve.

9

The Decline

THIS book has been concerned with Attic tragedy in the fifth century B.C. To this the present chapter is no more than a postscript. The later history of the Greek theatre, and of tragedy in particular, is certainly no less complex and problematic than the period already discussed: we now have far more material evidence—many theatre remains, large numbers of 'monuments'—but the essential primary sources of information, the plays, are lacking. In a few pages it is impossible even to outline the issues which this evidence, or lack of evidence, raises. We can only touch on some of the differences between the fifth century and what followed, in the hope that the contrast may throw into sharper relief the description already given of tragic drama at Athens in the time of the extant plays.

The theatre of Dionysus by the Acropolis continued in use until the fourth century A.D., undergoing the various changes and reconstructions which have left their mark on the site as we know it today. The festivals and dramatic contests went on, although the details of their later organisation are obscure. But the most striking development is the expansion of theatre activity, more or less on the Athenian model, beyond Attica until in time it reached every corner of the Greek-speaking world. In the fourth century or later scores of theatres were built—not only huge structures like those at Epidaurus or Megalopolis in the Peloponnese, or Pergamum near the Turkish coast, but others of various sizes to suit each community's needs. Even in the smallest town a theatre came to be regarded as a necessary public building. In these many theatres plays continued to be performed in their thousands in dramatic contests at local festivals—mostly in honour of Dionysus, but

129

sometimes for Apollo or some other god. To the regular festivals of local communities were added others, often far more splendid, financed by great patrons or set up in honour of princes and kings. For centuries drama and music in the theatre were the chief entertainment and the most popular form of culture throughout the Greek world.

In all this, tragedy had its full share. Because no plays and very few 'fragments' have survived, it must not be supposed that none were written. We know the names of many tragic poets and the titles of many of their works: the writing of tragedy, like the theatre, spread out from Athens, and flourished at Alexandria and elsewhere. Such a picture, it may be thought, hardly justifies the title of this chapter. Is not the conception of the fifth century B.C. as 'the great age of tragedy' mainly due to the chance that its products have reached us, whereas those of the fourth century and the Hellenistic period have not? Can tragedy fairly be said to have undergone a decline?

In quantity, no. The total aggregrate of productions staged, of audiences reached, of money spent, was clearly greater than ever before. It is when we turn to certain qualitative aspects of all this activity that we find significant changes which explain why the fifth century stands out.

One symptom is the Greeks' own glorification of fifth-century tragedy. When the Athenian statesman Lycurgus reconstructed the theatre of Dionysus in the second half of the fourth century with stone seating and a permanent stone *skene*, he ornamented it with statues of Aeschylus, Sophocles and Euripides; while about the same time, as we have seen, he established an authorised text of their plays. This canonisation of the three great tragic poets was reflected in the festival arrangements. The revival of earlier plays originally allowed as a compliment to Aeschylus was extended in the fourth century to Sophocles and Euripides as well, and the custom arose, perhaps from 386 B.C., for a tragedy by one of the three masters to be presented at each year's City

130

Dionysia as a prelude to the competition between new plays. Certainly this was a regular part of the programme by 341–339 B.C., when an inscription tells us that for three years in succession the playwright chosen was Euripides. In the Hellenistic age contests between actors performing fifth-century plays became normal at Athens and elsewhere. This ever-increasing emphasis on 'classical' tragedy may seem admirable, no more a sign of decline than the place given to Shakespeare in the theatre of today. But the cases are not parallel. The cult of fifth-century tragedy meant that a model was set up which must be copied by all but could be equalled by none. Although new versions of the old stories were produced and sometimes new themes were drawn from legend which do not appear among the fifth-century titles, creative adventure in the handling of living material seems to have been largely replaced by lifeless imitation of the past, and especially of Euripides. The rigidity of Lycurgus' stonework was matched by gradual ossification of the art of serious drama. It is not surprising that by A.D. 100 most productions were revivals, and a century later the creation of new plays had come to an end.

Some new plays, according to Aristotle (*Rhetoric* III, 12), were written for reading rather than performance. But the chief function of most of them (and of the revivals, too) was to provide material for the actor. His rising importance even in the fifth century is clear from the introduction of prizes for acting alongside the awards for plays. By Aristotle's time the actors' profession had far outstripped all others as the dominant element in the theatre, and we find the philosopher regretting (*Rhetoric* III, 1) that the actors now count for more than the playwrights. Leading actors toured the Greek world like the pop stars of today, receiving huge fees from states or wealthy patrons: Polus, the greatest star of the fourth century, is said to have been paid a talent for a two-day appearance. Small wonder that such nabobs of the theatre felt they had a right to alter or add to the author's text! Nor is it surprising that in time they consolidated their position by allying themselves together. From the third century B.C., if not earlier, actors along with other professional groups—poets, musicians, reciters, choral singers and trainers—formed guilds of Artists of Dionysus. These associations were locally based (one, for example, on Athens), but drew their membership from many places. There was keen rivalry between them, and now one, now another would be in the ascendant; but collectively they enjoyed a position of power and privilege unparalleled in theatre history. A guild could operate almost like an independent state, receiving and sending ambassadors. The privileges of its members could include exemption from military service, freedom from arrest, security of person and property. They were honoured and feasted, and on ceremonial public occasions marched in processions robed in purple and gold. The most popular actors became such international figures that their statues were set up in many places and they were given the citizenship of many cities. Eventually, in the first century A.D., a single association of Artists of Dionysus was organised throughout the Graeco-Roman world.

As fifth-century tragedy became the orthodox model and the actor emerged supreme, what changes took place in the presentation of the plays, the style and the mechanics of performance?

Once again it is impossible to separate two figures who are really the same person—the actor, ambitious to strengthen his reputation with his public, and the character he represents. To show off the actor's talents, every opportunity must be made (new authors, please note) for eloquent rhetoric and virtuoso song. But there was a subtler development than this: parallel with the ascendancy of the actor came the transformation of the role he played. The audience no longer saw traditional legend as a living reality. Its kings and queens had become creatures of another world, too distant to bear the semblance of normal humanity. Not only fifth-century tragedy must be glorified, but also its heroes and heroines. They must be made to *look* heroic—strange beings who no longer arouse pity and fear because for all their greatness they are somehow like ourselves, but wonder and horror because they are so remote.

Thus emerged the tragic hero, alias the renowned protagonist, in the form which confronted the Hellenistic audience and which we find in Hellenistic and Roman art. The change seems to have begun late in the fourth century B.C.; about the time when Lycurgus was rebuilding the theatre in stone, a new type of tragic mask came into use with unnaturally high forehead covered by a tower of hair. We cannot date with any certainty the other modifications which followed: the further distortion of the mask until it had an enormous forehead topped by close-packed ringlets, a gaping mouth, and staring eyes; the padding of chest and belly to swell the actor's bulk; the high-soled boot, eventually developed the ground.

Alongside this metamorphosis of the actor-hero came so far that it could raise him nine inches or more above the principal Hellenistic change in the structure of the theatre itself: the erection in front of the *skene* of a high stage raised perhaps twelve feet above the *orchestra*. Transference of the action to this level must have had the same effect as the alteration in the actor's appearance from the natural to the grotesque. The play and its characters now formed a separate world, probably more easily visible to the audience, but cut off from them by the twelve-foot drop. We are on the way to the proscenium arch theatre with its dichotomy of brightly lit stage and darkened auditorium. But here a difficult question arises, a historical problem parallel to the production problem faced by the producer of Greek tragedy today: when the high stage came into use, what was the function and the physical position of the chorus?

The shrinking of their part in the play during the fifth century led on, as we have seen, to the reduction of the choral ode to a mere interlude which might be completely irrelevant to the plot. A further step might have been the total disappearance of such inconvenient interruptions of the action. But it must be remembered that an increasing proportion of the tragedies presented were revivals, and in these the chorus could hardly have been eliminated even from the dialogue scenes, though its numbers may well have been reduced. Probably it was retained in new plays: certainly it reappeared in Roman tragedy. Its placing in the high-stage theatre is a puzzle to which various solutions have been proposed, but none of them entirely convincing—whether it joined the actors on the stage, as Vitruvius (V, 6) reports for the Roman theatre, or remained below them on the *orchestra* (the view adopted earlier in this book), or somehow moved between one level and the other. Whatever the answer, the chorus no longer provided a bridge between actors and audience, or had the effect of bringing all present in the theatre together into a single whole.

Greek tragedy of the fifth century B.C. has been portrayed in this book as the product of the sovereign city-state in its heyday, part of a great public occasion which was organised by the people's own representatives and financed by the city from its revenues and by wealthy citizens; a mass gathering which brought together hundreds of the citizens as active participants and many thousands as an audience closely involved in all that they saw and heard; a political event much concerned with the glory of Athens; a religious ritual in which all took part. The picture becomes clearer by contrast with the sequel, so imitative of the past yet in some ways so different. Towards the end of the fourth century B.C. the *choregoi* ceased to exist at Athens, and the running of the dramatic festivals there and in other cities was entrusted to a festival organiser (Greek: *agonothetes*) provided with funds by the state. We know little of how he worked at Athens or elsewhere, but he must have gone beyond the local community to draw upon the general supply of professional talent no longer attached to any particular place; no doubt the guilds of the Artists of Dionysus had some part in the arrangements. The festival itself remained a great civic occasion, but with significant differences. After the Macedonian conquest

134

the glory of the city could count for little, although much might be made of the glory of a royal patron. Ritual could continue as a formality, but had lost much of its earlier significance. The public came together for entertainment—above all, as we have seen, to watch and wonder at the strange figures of the actors on the high stage as they played the roles of the heroes and heroines of the far distant past.

In contrast with the fifth century this later trend and its results may well be called a decline, compared with which the age of Aeschylus, Sophocles and Euripides stands out as a unique phase in theatre history, the product of a situation unparalleled in more recent times. In our own day technology has made it possible to overcome one of the main differences between the modern and the ancient world—the vast size of the modern community. The microphone has enabled the human voice to reach mass audiences far larger than those who crowded the benches at Athens and Epidaurus. Television has overcome the impossibility of assembling the whole community together by bringing the performer (and again it is he who chiefly matters) into every home. But it is not the function of this book to draw questionable analogies or seek dubious conclusions about the state of the theatre today. The reader must form his own reflections on the situation and prospects of drama in the twentieth century in comparison with the achievement of fifth-century Athens.

Bibliography

THE number of books and articles on all aspects of Greek tragedy is very large. This list contains only a small selection of those available in English. Extensive bibliographies will be found in the books asterisked below; and a survey of publications on all aspects of the subject will be found in *Fifty Years (and Twelve) of Classical Scholarship* (Oxford, Basil Blackwell, 1968), pp. 88–122.

FESTIVALS, THEATRE, PERFORMANCE

P. D. Arnott, *An Introduction to the Greek Theatre* (London, Macmillan, 1959; Bloomington, Indiana University Press, paperback, 1963). A simple account of theatre and plays for the general reader.

P. D. Arnott, *Greek Scenic Conventions in the Fifth Century B.C.* (Oxford University Press, 1962). A detailed discussion of the acting area, settings, properties and machinery.

*M. Bieber, *The History of the Greek and Roman Theatre* (Princeton University Press, 1939; 2nd edition, 1961). Chiefly valuable as a full collection of the visual evidence for all phases of theatre history in antiquity.

I. Brooke, *Costume in Greek Classic Drama* (London, Methuen, 1962; New York, Theatre Arts). A practical guide illustrated with the author's own drawings.

A. M. Dale, *Collected Papers* (Cambridge University Press, 1969). Includes several valuable articles on the staging of tragedy.

V. Ehrenberg, *The People of Aristophanes* (Oxford, Basil Blackwell, 1943; 2nd edition, 1962; New York, Schocken Books). The evidence of comedy for life and theatre-going in late fifth-century Athens.

R. C. Flickinger, *The Greek Theater and its Drama* (Chicago University Press, 1918; 4th edition 1936, reprinted 1965). Greek drama explained through its environment. Detailed discussion of technical problems.

BIBLIOGRAPHY

A. E. Haigh, *The Attic Theatre* (Oxford University Press, 1889; 3rd edition revised by A. W. Pickard-Cambridge, 1907; New York, Haskell House, 1968). Still useful in part, but out of date on many aspects.

N. C. Hourmouziades, *Production and Imagination in Euripides* (Athens, 1965). Euripides' use of the theatre and its machinery.

*A. W. Pickard-Cambridge, *The Theatre of Dionysus in Athens* (London & New York, Oxford University Press, 1946). The standard work, fully documented and illustrated, on the history of this theatre down to the Roman Empire.

*A. W. Pickard-Cambridge, *The Dramatic Festivals of Athens* (London & New York, Oxford University Press, 1953; 2nd edition revised by J. Gould and D. M. Lewis, 1968). A well documented and illustrated survey of our information about the festivals, actors, chorus and audience.

G. M. Sifakis, *Studies in the History of Hellenistic Drama* (University of London, Athlone Press, 1967; New York, Oxford University Press). Mainly concerned with Delos and Delphi. Valuable appendix on later treatment of the chorus.

T. B. L. Webster, *Greek Theatre Production* (London, Methuen, 1956; 2nd edition, 1970). Mainly concerned with evidence for costumes, masks and scenery in all centres down to late Hellenistic period.

T. B. L. Webster, *Monuments Illustrating Tragedy and Satyr Play* (Bulletin of Institute of Classical Studies, London, Suppl. 14, 1962). Lists and discusses visual evidence for actors and masks.

T. B. L. Webster, *The Greek Chorus* (London, Methuen, 1970). A review of the archaeological and metrical evidence for choral dancing of all periods. Too technical for the general reader.

PLAYWRIGHTS AND PLAYS

General

A. M. Dale, *The Lyric Metres of Greek Drama* (London & New York, Cambridge University Press, 1948; 2nd edition, 1968).

J. Jones, *On Aristotle and Greek Tragedy* (London, Chatto & Windus, 1962; New York, Oxford University Press, 1962; paperback, Oxford University Press, 1968). Difficult reading, but breaks much new ground.

H. D. F. Kitto, *Greek Tragedy: a Literary Study* (London, Methuen, 1939; 3rd edition, 1961; New York, Barnes & Noble, paperback, 1969).

H. D. F. Kitto, *Form and Meaning in Drama: a Study of Six Greek Plays and of Hamlet* (London, Methuen, 1956; New York, Barnes & Noble).

R. Lattimore, *The Poetry of Greek Tragedy* (Baltimore, Johns Hopkins Press, 1958).

R. Lattimore, *Story Patterns in Greek Tragedy* (University of London, Athlone Press, 1964; University of Michigan Press, paperback, 1969).

A. Lesky, *Greek Tragedy,* translated from the German by H. A. Frankfort (London, Ernest Benn, 1965; New York, Barnes & Noble, paperback).

D. W. Lucas, *The Greek Tragic Poets* (London, Cohen & West, 1950; 2nd edition, 1959; New York, Norton, paper-back).

B. Snell, *The Discovery of the Mind,* translated from the German by T. G. Rosenmeyer (Oxford, Basil Blackwell, 1953; New York, Harper & Row Torch Book, paperback). Especially Ch. 5, 'Myth and Reality in Greek Tragedy'.

A. W. Pickard-Cambridge, *Dithyramb, Tragedy and Comedy* (London & New York, Oxford University Press, 1927; 2nd edition, revised and enlarged by T. B. L. Webster, 1962). A well-documented study of the origins of drama.

Aeschylus

G. G. A. Murray, *Aeschylus, the Creator of Tragedy* (Lon-

don & New York, Oxford University Press, 1940; paperback
edition, 1962).

G. Thomson, *Aeschylus and Athens: a Study in the Social
Origins of Drama* (London, Lawrence and Wishart, 1941;
2nd edition, 1948; New York, Grosset & Dunlap, 3rd
edition, 1969, paperback).

Sophocles
C. M. Bowra, *Sophoclean Tragedy* (London & New York,
Oxford University Press, 1944; paperback edition, 1965).

A. J. A. Waldock, *Sophocles the Dramatist* (London & New
York, Cambridge University Press, 1951; paperback
edition, 1966).

T. B. L. Webster, *An Introduction to Sophocles* (Oxford
University Press, 1936; 2nd edition, 1969; New York,
Barnes & Noble, paperback).

Euripides
D. J. Conacher, *Euripidean Drama: Myth, Theme and
Structure* (Toronto University Press, 1967).

G. M. A. Grube, *The Drama of Euripides* (London,
Methuen, 1941).

G. G. A. Murray, *Euripides and his Age* (London, Williams
& Norgate, 1913; 2nd edition, Oxford University Press,
1946; paperback, 1965).

T. B. L. Webster, *The Tragedies of Euripides* (London,
Methuen, 1967; New York, Barnes & Noble). Largely
concerned with the lost plays.

TEXTS AND TRANSLATIONS

The Greek text of all the extant tragedies of Aeschylus,
Sophocles and Euripides is included in the Oxford Classical
Texts series, published by the Oxford University Press. The
Loeb Classical Library (W. Heinemann Ltd.) gives the
Greek text of all the plays with English translation opposite.
The standard collection of 'fragments' is *Tragicorum
Graecorum Fragmenta* edited by A. Nauck (2nd edition
Leipzig, 1889; revised with supplement by B. Snell, Hilde-

sheim, 1964). 'Fragments' recovered from papyri are given in *Select Papyri* Vol. III, edited by D. L. Page (Loeb Classical Library, revised edition, 1962).

Aeschylus, Euripides and some plays of Sophocles were notably translated by Gilbert Murray, but most modern readers find the style of his versions no longer acceptable. Translations of all the tragedies are included in Everyman's Library (Dent, London), and most of them are available in the Penguin Classics. Perhaps the most successful modern versions are *The Complete Greek Tragedies,* nine volumes edited by D. Grene and R. Lattimore (Chicago University Press, 1953–59). A selection is provided in a three-volume edition. Anthologies of extracts from the tragedies are to be found in *The Oxford Book of Greek Verse in Translation* and *Greek Drama for Everyman*, by F. L. Lucas (London, Dent, 1954; New York, Viking Press, paperback, 1968, retitled: *Greek Tragedy & Comedy*).

Aristotle's *Poetics.* The latest English edition is by D. W. Lucas (Oxford University Press, 1968). For a translation, see T. S. Dorsch's version in *Classical Literary Criticism* (Penguin Classics).

Index

Main references are italicised. References to works are given under their authors.

Pronunciation of Greek words. The letter *e* is always a sign of a new syllable, unlike the *e* in *bone*. It is either short, as in *met*, or long, as in *mēte*. In Greek words in this index long *e* and *o* are marked *ē* and *ō*, and a hyphen is sometimes used to show division between syllables.

INDEX